NANTUCKET

Portrait of an American Town

PHOTOGRAPHY AND TEXT
BY MARY HAFT

Windcliff Press
Nantucket, Massachusetts

First Edition © 2008 by Mary Haft

Art Direction by Roberto Sablayrolles

Graphic Design by Eduardo Garcia

Edited by Elizabeth Oldham

Library of Congress Cataloging-in-Publication
Data available

ISBN: 978-0-9815828-0-1

Printed in China

WWW.NANTUCKETPORTRAIT.COM

P R E F A C E

There are moments that define a sense of place and a sense of time. Occasionally, those moments mark a shock of recognition that a landscape you have loved could be lost.

Early one Thursday morning, several years ago, happily ensconced at my favorite spot at the lunch counter of the Nantucket Pharmacy, reading the just published *Inquirer and Mirror,* the island's weekly newspaper, I read with alarm the front-page headline about Bartlett's Ocean View Farm. At first glance, I thought the farm would be sold. But closer reading revealed that the Bartlett Family had reached an agreement with the Nantucket Land Council for the purchase of a conservation restriction on over one hundred acres, with an agreement that this land would continue to be farmed, much as it had for generations of this family. By preserving the farm as agricultural ground, this sense of place would be protected. But in that moment, the imprint of loss felt real. And suddenly, it mattered to try to capture and document what I have loved before it is lost.

The years have wrought much change on this tiny island, a windswept isle some

thirty miles out to sea. Twenty years ago, there were around four thousand year-round residents; to-day, islanders number closer to ten thousand. Summer brings with it the necessary fuel of tourism, but with it the crowds that threaten to extinguish that which we love. Nearly forty thousand visitors, arriving in some ten thousand cars (thousands more arriving by plane or ferry) strain the capacity of the island's natural resources. As many have bought increasingly expensive vacation homes, Nantucket has had to adjust to a new economic reality: many islanders can no longer afford to live here.

The landscape has changed, a sensibility has shifted, landmarks that we took for granted have disappeared. *Nothing Gold Can Stay,* as poet Robert Frost's words evocatively speak to the idea that a place that you have known and loved for years can be altered: by time, by circumstance, and by that steady march of an advancing world. Nantucket: home to generations of islanders, loved by generations of families, a name that carries a host of memories and a history that resonates through time.

That was the genesis of this idea: to capture an island that is unique in the world and to hold on to what is precious to so many of us—the spirit of Nantucket. For beneath the façade of this beautiful resort destination beats the heart of a small town.

WALKING THROUGH HISTORY
CHAPTER ONE

Authenticity resonates through this tiny island. Walk down Main Street, its cobblestones brought over from the mainland to pave the thoroughfare rendered rutted and muddy by heavy carts carrying whale oil to outlying refineries. From Caton Circle at the top of Main down to Straight Wharf, buildings that have stood for generations and weathered great change continue to grace this community. Thanks to the extraordinary efforts of the Nantucket Land Bank, the Nantucket Land Council, the Conservation Foundation, and several other preservation agencies, large parcels of land seem unchanged. Craggy, windswept moors; acres of cranberry bogs, and miles of coastline all beckon to what life had been and continues to be—a call of the wild and a reminder of the continuity of living history.

Listen for a moment as dawn breaks or in late afternoon when fog creeps in, as the foghorn at the East Jetty sounds its plaintive warning—a call that feels centuries old, a pause that is as ephemeral as the wind and just as haunting. Windsong is a constant, from gentle breezes that bring sounds of the sea and island life to a wind that picks up force until it reaches a shrieking, howling pitch.

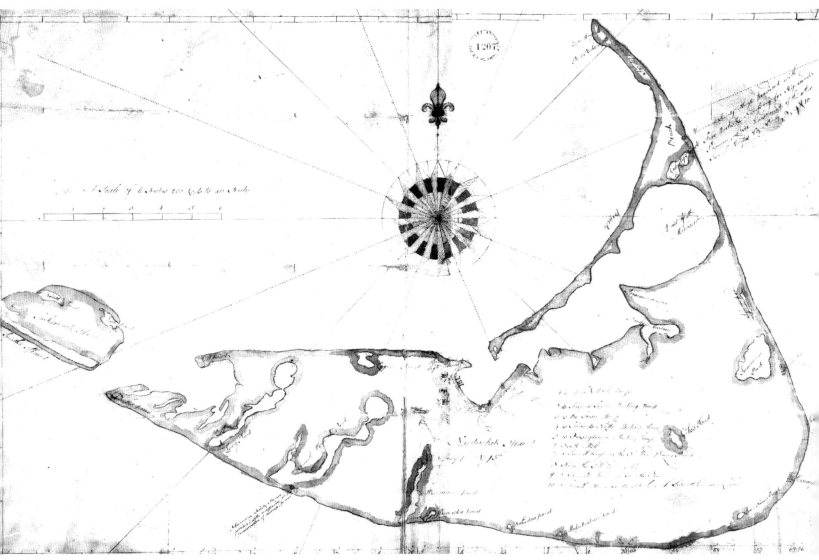

Nantucket Island, May 1, 1795. Photocopy of hand drawn map in Massachusetts State Archives.

Nantucket! Take out your map and look at it. See what a real corner of the world it occupies;
how it stands there, away offshore . . . a mere hillock, elbow of sand; all beach without
a background.

Herman Melville, *Moby-Dick*

Nantucket weaves its past from many stories, tracing its beginnings to a tribe of Indians known as the Wampanoag, who had been here for centuries before the English arrived in the early 1600s. Tribal folklore carries the legend of the Indian giant, Moshup, a benevolent presence who shared the remains of his gigantic meals with the tribes that stayed near. In gratitude, they made him a gift of their entire tobacco crop. After a leisurely smoke, Moshup scattered the ashes on the sea, creating the fog that frequently surrounds the island. Even today, the fog here is called "Moshup's smoke."

On the "Far-Away Isle," as the Indians dubbed Nantucket, it was a hardy existence. The island's location, so far out at sea, was literally a world away from the mainland skirmishes between the Puritan English settlers and other European arrivals, as well as a separation from the divisions that were plaguing the Native American populations. On Nantucket, Native American life was a rich tapestry of tribal traditions and folklore, daily work that was embedded with the earth and the sea, and fraught with the tensions between tribes in the eastern sector of the island and those to the west.

Native Americans were a critical factor in what was to become Nantucket's primary activity and source of income—the whaling industry, which would transform the island into a major seaport and open trading pathways to the larger world. Adept at maneuvering their dugout canoes through Nantucket waters, physically strong and agile, the Indians were a ready source of the manpower necessary, indeed, indispensable, to the settlers. Employment arrangements were not always equitable, however, fueled as they were by the English who were not above subjugating the Indians to a form of indentured servitude, almost akin to slavery. Also, the natives' alcohol consumption, entirely foreign to their culture, had dire consequences.

It is the legacy of American history that the lives and livelihoods of American Indians were lost as the English settlers made their way across Indian lands. The New England seacoast was settled in much the same way as the rest of America: virtual eradication of the Indian population by wars, introduced diseases, and seizure of their hunting and farming territories.

Evocative names remain: Quidnet, Monomoy, Sesachacha Pond, Siasconset, Wauwinet, Coskata, Coatue—all that is left of the American Indian legacy on the island.

Nantucket's remote location helped to ensure its isolation from the Puritan colonists who were settling New England. First charted by Captain Bartholomew Gosnold on a navigational voyage in 1602, Nantucket remained in native hands until 1642, when Thomas Mayhew, of Watertown, Massachusetts, negotiated an arrangement to acquire both Martha's Vineyard and Nantucket. The Puritan practice of punishing those with social and religious differences, including people of the Baptist faith, gave rise particularly to the persecution of Quakers, members of a relatively new religious sect. That intolerance, along with some economic incentives, have been suggested as contributing elements to the story of how Nantucket was bought by yet another party. In 1659, Thomas Macy, Tristram Coffin, Richard Swain, and Edward Starbuck, along with five others, bought the island from Thomas Mayhew, and are considered today to be the "Founding Fathers" of Nantucket.

Dorcas Honorable (1776–1855)
Photographic portrait of the last
known Indian woman of Nantucket.

Abram Quary (1772–1854)
Photographic portrait of the last
known Indian man on Nantucket, ca. 1840.

Quarterly Meeting Day, 1890s.
Whittemore Gardner driving and Amy Gardner.

QUAKERISM ON NANTUCKET

The Religious Society of Friends, whose members are commonly called Quakers, is a deeply personal, intensely spiritual brand of Christianity that was formed in the chrysalis of faith that sprang from the repressive Protestantism that caused many to flee seventeenth-century England. Essentially, Friends honor individual faith and an individual's capacity to seek and to find a personal relationship with God. Powered by the belief that each person carries the divine light within, it is the collective power of shared communion where Quaker faith shines most brightly: God's grace made real by human intention brought forth in the weekly "meeting for worship."

Quaker Meeting House

Nantucket became a safe haven for the first settlers; freedom from fear and persecution formed a central tenet of faith. Personal choice and free will became part of the fabric of life on Nantucket, and the Society of Friends grew as an increasingly significant element of that life, along with several other Christian denominations.

From its beginnings around 1700, a few families, led by Mary Starbuck, laid the foundation of the island's Quaker community, which by the 1720s had grown to number several hundred families. Nantucket's political, economic, and social structure came to be dominated by Quakers. They began as farmers and sheepherders, maintaining the crops to feed their families and raising sheep for the cultivation of wool, a vital industry in colonial America.

Nantucketers also looked to the sea as a natural part of survival, as island waters abounded in fish and shellfish. Shortly after the settlers' arrival, in what was to be a fortuitous turn, a species of small whales occasionally washed ashore, and the hardy islanders would strip the carcasses of blubber and process it to extract the valuable oil.   By 1690, they had equipped small boats to fish the offshore waters and bring the whales in, thus creating the whaling industry on Nantucket.

Larger boats began longer voyages, primarily in pursuit of the northern right whale and the humpback. Whaling had gained its hold on the island.

First page of Thomas Nickerson's manuscript account of his voyage aboard the ship *Essex*: "My First Voyage at Sea and subsequent loss of the ship *Essex*."

THE WHALING CAPITAL OF THE WORLD

Around 1712, Nantucketers had their first encounter with the great sperm whale (later to become legendary in Herman Melville's classic, *Moby-Dick*). A creature of enormous proportions, it was pursued for the superior quality and quantity of its oil and the highly valued spermaceti contained in its great head. But this whale inhabited deep water, so larger boats were needed to go out on longer journeys and would tow the immense creatures back to shore for processing. It was only a matter of time before the necessity of creating oil-processing vessels at sea became part of maritime life. Whaling enterprises required capital to fund the larger vessels that were required for these lengthy journeys. By 1760, most of the smaller ships had been replaced by self-contained factories, with on-board tryworks capable of processing blubber into oil to be stored in a hold filled with barrels and carrying a supply of food to last the four or five months it would take for the completion of a successful voyage.

Eighteenth-century Quakers played a vital role in the development of Nantucket as a whaling empire, in no small part due to the network of Quaker communities in the larger world. Ties of faith, friendship, and marriage created links to other maritime centers, such as Newport, Rhode Island, and New Bedford and Salem, Massachusetts. Sailing vessels could come to port in European capitals and find their Quaker counterparts.

70

"Skinning whale to get the blubber."

Tragedy was never far from any tale of whaling misadventures, and none more so than that of Captain George Pollard Jr. and his ship, the Essex. In 1820, on a voyage to the Pacific, having spent months at sea and battered by raging storms, this ship was attacked by a monstrous sperm whale. Deliberately and with intent, the whale charged in two separate strikes. As the Essex was sinking, the captain and crew clambered aboard the ship's small whaleboats, and drifted in the open sea for three months until they were rescued. Ultimately, they faced their only chance of survival by living off the flesh of their companions. Drawing straws, the short straw fell to the captain's own nephew, Owen Coffin. By the time of their rescue, only eight of the original crew of twenty had survived.

The tragic tale came to the attention of author Herman Melville, who, hearing the harrowing story, brought truth to fiction and produced the American literary classic, *Moby-Dick*, published in 1851. Returning to the origins of this classic American epic, writer Nathaniel Philbrick brought this survival story to life with his book *In the Heart of the Sea: The Tragedy of the Whaleship Essex*, published in 2000.

Whaling ship *California*, 1842.
Nantucket Historical Association

By the early 1800s, voyages had lengthened to several years. The business of whaling infiltrated the entire island. Most had some hand in its process, from seamen to merchants, as ancillary services sprang up—from building ships and wharves to the servicing of cargo and the prodigious production of candles from the spermaceti wax—all contributing to the success of the industry, as wealth and exotic foreign goods poured in. As so many of the island's men and boys were at sea, women began to play a greater role in the island's economic and social circles. They managed family affairs and, increasingly, established their own commercial enterprises in the town.

Unusual for its time, the Quaker faith adhered to founder George Fox's creed of the equality of men and women, and that modern view found its place in this small whaling capitol of the world.

In the late 1750s, the Quaker population stood at 1,173. The Great Meeting House had been enlarged with additions made in 1764 so that two thousand people, a majority of Nantucket's population, could be seated for meetings. Nantucket was a bustling, cosmopolitan, sophisticated society, with goods being traded from around the world, and with news from ports near and far making their way to this small island thirty miles out to sea.

This prosperous period could not last. The whaling industry itself was changing. Oil from Nantucket vessels was being offloaded directly in ports like Newport and other coastal cities, including New Bedford, that had access to the developing railroads. By the 1850s, kerosene was being processed from petroleum, a cheaper and more easily available product than labor-intensive spermaceti oil. War took its toll; the Seven Years' War, better known in America as the French and Indian War, in the

Rare illustrated log of the ship *Susan* on its fifth voyage to
the Pacific Ocean, December 1841 through May 1846. One
illustration depicts a Nantucket Sleighride (harpooned whale
towing a whaleboat); the other shows Captain Reuben Russell
riding on a whale's tail.

BOARDING KNIVES

When the huge strip of blubber was hoisted in the air above the deck, a boarding knife cut it down into smaller blanket pieces. Boarding knives were double-edged blades mounted on short wooden handles, with a Turk's-head knot in the middle to prevent hands from sliding onto the blade.

SINGLE-FLUE HARPOON

The single-flue harpoon was developed in the 1820s as an improvement on the double-flue harpoon. After the head of the single-flue harpoon had entered the whale's body, the force of the line bent its shaft, causing the single head to fasten in the whale's flesh. The broad flat side of the harpoon head pressed against the uncut flesh, making it difficult to dislodge.

THE BLUBBER HOOK: HOISTING THE "BLANKET PIECE"

The giant blubber hook was used to hoist the six-foot-wide strips of blubber, called "blanket pieces," onto the deck of the whaleship for processing into smaller pieces. The massive hook was attached to a line connected to the mast by the ship's windlass. Once on deck, the blubber pieces were transferred into the "blubber room," a space below deck where large pieces of blubber were cut into smaller pieces for trying-out.

WHALING PROCESS

View of men on suspended catwalk, cutting in on a sperm whale at the side of the whaling vessel.

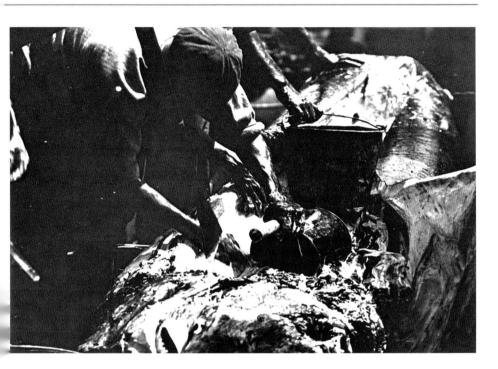

Bailing the oil from the head case of a whale.

Text and images courtesy of the Nantucket Historical Association and the NHA Whaling Museum.

MINCING KNIVES

Once boarded on deck, the blanket pieces of blubber were cut into smaller "horse-pieces" using boarding knives. These were then transferred to a "mincing horse," a kind of chopping station by the tryworks, where they were cut with mincing knives into thin slices known as "bible leaves" for easier boiling.

FIRE IN THE CHIMNEY!

To kill a whale, the officer drove the lance into the "life" of the animal, a region near its lungs, causing it to spout blood. A shout of "fire in the chimney!" alerted the whalers that their prey was entering its death flurry.

HEAD-CASE BUCKET

To remove spermaceti from the sperm whale's head, a young and agile crew member was lowered into the head case attached by his waist to a "monkey rope" with a bucket in hand. If the case was split open on deck, oil poured out and covered the whalemen up to their knees.

TRYWORKS OPERATION AND TOOLS

Tryworks were made of two iron pots set in brick furnaces, with pans of water underneath to prevent the deck of the ship from burning. Two fuel doors below the pots allowed access to the fires, which were fueled with wood and scraps of whale fritters from previous sessions. Once blubber had been rendered into oil, it was bailed into two copper cooling tanks at the tryworks' sides prior to removal to casks for storage. The blubber pike and blubber fork were used to manipulate the scarves of blubber on deck, and to pitch the bible leaves into the trypots.

SKIMMER - When the bible leaves of blubber had rendered their oil, the remaining parts, known as "fritters," were removed from the trypots with a large pierced skimmer that allowed excess oil to pour back into the pots.

BAILER - When the oil in the trypots had boiled sufficiently, it was removed with a large ladle called a bailer and poured into the copper cooling tanks attached to the sides of the tryworks.

QUANTITIES OF OIL FROM THE SPERM WHALE

The oil harvested from a sperm whale consisted of the oil from the head case, called "sperm oil," and the body blubber, called "whale oil." A large female sperm whale might give up 35 barrels of oil, while the largest bulls could yield 70 to 90 barrels. When a whale was spotted, the captain might cry out, "Thar blows, she's an eighty-barreler, lads!" Since the typical whale-oil barrel measured an industry standard 31½ gallons, a large sperm whale could yield nearly 2,800 gallons. Records of head-case sizes alone indicate that a head case could yield anywhere from 15 to 30 barrels of spermaceti, or roughly 470 to 950 gallons!

WHALING PROCESS

Trypots boiling on the deck of a ship.

The whaling vessel *Wanderer,* trying out, boiling whale blubber, at night, to all appearances like a ship ablaze.

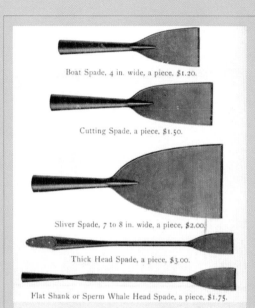

Boat Spade, 4 in. wide, a piece, $1.20.

Cutting Spade, a piece, $1.50.

Sliver Spade, 7 to 8 in. wide, a piece, $2.00.

Thick Head Spade, a piece, $3.00.

Flat Shank or Sperm Whale Head Spade, a piece, $1.75.

WHALING SPADES

Boat Spade -The boat spade cut the first holes in the whale to fasten the towing line with a chain after the whale was killed.

CUTTING SPADE - *Cutting spades, mounted on extremely long spruce poles, made the initial zig-zag cuts in the blubber from the cutting stage above.*

SLIVER SPADE - *The broad sliver spades decapitated the whale by severing the pieces of flesh and blubber, known as "slivers," that connected the head and the body.*

THROAT, OR HEAD, SPADE - *Throat, or head, spades cut passages in the head of the whale to secure a chain to the whale's head.*

Text and images courtesy of the Nantucket Historical Association and the NHA Whaling Museum.

CASK FACTS AND FIGURES

Whale-oil casks were made of fine white oak and came in all shapes and sizes, from enormous ten-barrel tuns to long and sleek four-barrel casks. The term "barrel" was a unit of measurement equal to 31½ gallons and did not refer to a physical barrel. A successful whaling voyage returned 1,000–2,000 barrels of oil, which would be stored in several hundred casks packed into the hold. Once a whaleship returned to port, its casks were unloaded onto the dock, opened, and the oil measured for quantity and quality.

"We are now 40 days out and the cooper has made but 3 boat buckets, one lantern keg, sawed off 3 boat kegs and made one grindstone tub. All of which a good cooper would have made in 3 days."

Log of the *Harvest*
SEPTEMBER 21, 1853

Coopers were skilled artisans who created casks, barrels, tubs, and kegs of all sizes to hold whale oil and ship provisions. At the beginning of a whaling voyage, curved barrel staves were stacked tightly and stored in the hold until assembled by the ships' cooper. During the journey, especially if a whale was sighted, the cooper would put together giant casks by fitting the staves together in the grooved wooden base, sometimes using reeds between staves for caulking.

View of rows of whale oil barrels stored on a wharf. Four men are pouring oil through funnels into the casks – most likely "topping off" the barrels.

Crewmen on deck of the *California*, cutting up whale pieces for the tryworks.

GREASY FACTS AND FIGURES

Whale oil was stored on board in casks of all shapes and sizes, with different barrel capacities.

The barrel was an abstract unit of measurement equaling 31½ gallons, not a physical container on board. Oil was stored in wooden casks varying in shape and size, designed to take advantage of every nook and cranny in the whaleship's hold. Large casks could hold up to ten barrels, while long, narrow casks, called "shooks," typically stored 3–5 barrels. Casks were marked "S.O." for sperm, and "W.O." for whale oil. On "greasy," or successful, voyages, whalers typically brought home 1,000–2,000 barrels of sperm oil, the most valuable of all oils. Whaleships were constructed broad in the beam, with huge holds below for "hauling down" as many casks as possible. The record catch of oil was logged by the Nantucket ship *Sarah*, Frederick Arthur master, which brought back an unprecedented 3,490 barrels of sperm oil from her 1827 voyage to the Pacific Ocean.

Text and images courtesy of the Nantucket Historical Association and the NHA Whaling Museum.

Aboard the schooner, *Ellen A. Swift*: Group portrait of sea captains, including Captain George Dunham (second from left), lost when the *Ellen A. Swift* disappeared.

"And thus have these naked Nantucketers, these sea-hermits, issuing from their anthill in the sea, overrun and conquered the world like so many Alexanders."

Herman Melville, *Moby-Dick*

mid-eighteenth century reached its long arm into Nantucket waters: it was reported that "…seventy-one Nantucket Whaling sloops were taken by the French and a number of ships and crews had to be ransomed from their French captors." In 1763, when Britain defeated France, a revolutionary era began. Out of the catalyst of regional and global war, came the American Revolution, and the United States of America was born with the Declaration of Independence on July 4, 1776—Great Britain recognizing that independence with the Treaty of Paris in 1783.

Affected significantly by the War of 1812, Nantucket's whaling industry revived and flourished until the mid-1830s and struggled on for another decade, until the Great Fire of 1846 wrought its havoc. Another event, the Gold Rush of 1849 lured hundreds of Nantucket men and boys to California to seek their fortunes. The death blow to Nantucket's economy came with the Civil War, which claimed the lives of seventy-three of the four hundred men who served in it.

The political, economic, and social consequence of war and the realities of a changing world economy, along with the diminishing Quaker population, created crippling change for the island. Once a bustling seaport, with a thriving economy, it now languished. Its whaling days were over. As the life of the island ebbed away, so did its people. By 1870, the once booming town with a population of ten thousand had been reduced to four thousand residents.

Nantucket's geography played its part in the creation of what had been a Quaker stronghold. The sea provided a natural containment for the ideals and founding vision that had taken hold. It was a community that unified around a common goal of the spiritual and practical principles of the universal attainment of Truth. Quakerism's guiding principles and dedication to simplicity profoundly influenced Nantucket's architecture, manner of dress, and social mores. Once lost, never again would Quakerism find itself at the center of life as it had on the island of Nantucket.

THE RISE OF A NEW INDUSTRY: TOURISM

The waters that enclose Nantucket had provided sustenance through almost three centuries of seafaring; the sea would help to usher in a new tide: tourism. Having failed to establish an economy based on agriculture or industry, following the demise of whaling and the loss of all related business, Nantucket foundered. Struggling to find its financial footing, the town began to advertise the benefits of healthy living. A seaside holiday would be just the refreshment to lure a weary city dweller to these shores. Advertisements began to appear in mainland publications, and resourceful housewives opened their homes to boarders—early "bed & breakfasts," to be followed by inns and resorts, all catering to the burgeoning business of tourism. Although boarding houses certainly existed at the height of the whaling days, the new trade was all about the benefits of the sand and sea and the cool ocean breezes. It was only the beginning of an entrepreneurial spirit that would infuse the island with new hopes and new prospects.

The Ocean View House in Siasconset

The town of Nantucket, as we know it today, echoes its past, but not its beginnings. Nantucket's earliest English settlers established a village along the north shore of the island at Capaum, where the small natural harbor became the port of entry for maritime trade on Nantucket. The village of Sherburne grew up around this harbor, a settlement that expanded to incorporate some sixty families.

By the early 1720s, action of the tides and currents had silted up the harbor entrance—a circumstance that led to the settlers moving, some with their houses, to the larger, or "Great Harbor," several miles eastward. This move created the sense of town that we enjoy today. The new town was organized around the harbor, with small lots linking villagers, connected by walking paths and lanes, creating a more cohesive sense of community. In 1723, Richard Macy, grandson of one of Nantucket's original settlers, began construction of a wharf that was to usher in a new day of commerce. Considered a master builder, Macy built a wharf that extended straight into the harbor from Main Street, layering the structure with logs and rocks buried deep into the muddy, sandy bottom. Straight Wharf became the

"Not far away, ———
we saw
The strange, old-fashioned
silent
Town,

The wooden houses,
quaint
and brown."
Longfellow

Old North Wharf and Steamboat Wharf 1892.
Old postcard with two photos and script.

anchor for the new town. Centrally located and easily accessible, the harbor became the hub of shipping, reaching its apex at the height of the whaling days.

It wasn't until 1795 that the town was named Nantucket, taken from the name of the island in the language of the Wampanoag, which has been translated as "the land far out to sea." Another source has nai-an-tuck-et, meaning "tidal run around a sharp corner," which describes the point of the island that separates Nantucket Harbor from Nantucket Sound.

Throughout the late 1700s and much of the 1800s, Nantucket was a bustling seaport, with Straight Wharf as the center of the thriving whaling industry, goods and services being purveyed from several more wharves built on either side. The waterfront itself wasn't the pristine harbor we see today. Imagine the docks loaded with casks of oil, ships leaking their smelly cargoes, candle factories and cooper-ages, ship chandleries and oil warehouses, blacksmiths and boat builders, along with boarding houses and fishing shanties.

Imagine the ships heading out into the Atlantic Ocean and, later, in the whaling heyday, going farther afield around the Horn into the Pacific. With the advent of the China trade, owners of returning vessels laden with porcelains and exotic art and furniture, silks, and other opulent textiles would find ready buyers in the wealthy whaling families who had built mansions along the upper reaches of Main Street and at the highest points of Orange Street, looking out to the busy harbor and the wharves.

The town was a hub of activity, with clothing shops and a variety of markets for food and dry goods. With many of the men of Nantucket occupied in the whaling trade, the women of the town managed many of the businesses and were active in politics—circumstances endorsed by the Quaker faith, which celebrated equality

Town and Harbor of Nantucket from a Survey by Lieutenant Colonel J. Anderson, Topographical Engineer, 1826

Shopkeepers of Petticoat Row, 1885.

Photographic portrait of Maria Mitchell (ca. fifty years old).

of both the spirit and the sexes. With women taking center stage in commerce, the string of shops along Centre Street, whose proprietors were all women, was dubbed Petticoat Row, and it became a meeting place for shopkeepers and shoppers alike.

At the juncture of Main Street and Centre Street, the Pacific National Bank, built in 1818, stands tall. At the time the town's leading financial institution, it recalls the past glories of the whaling empire, whose voyages it financed and whose name conjures up the vast riches garnered in the Pacific Ocean.

Just outside the bank's side entrance on Main Street, down the steps to the left, there is a marker of a different sort—a three-foot-high Meridian Stone, pointed at the top like a pyramid, and identical to another such stone marker a little way up Fair Street, in front of the Nantucket Historical Association's Research Library. The two markers were placed in 1840 by William Mitchell, father of Maria Mitchell, America's first woman astronomer, and an astronomer himself. The stones were used by surveyors, who would align the markers in their quadrants to establish true north in order to ascertain the precise parameters of lot lines.

Maria Mitchell provides a way to connect the dots between historic institutions and individuals who have found their place in history. Born in 1818, she was a daughter of a profoundly accomplished mathematician, amateur astronomer, and educator and learned at her father's side, helping him in the preparation of nautical almanacs and regulating navigational instruments used on whaling ships. William Mitchell was for a time cashier of the Pacific Bank, an executive position, and the Mitchell family lived in quarters above the bank. William Mitchell installed a small telescope in an observatory on the roof of the bank, through which, on the

Downtown Nantucket, including Main Street and the harbor, 1860s.

Portrait of six unidentified men, 1860s.

first night of October 1847, Maria spied what she believed was a new comet. Knowing the Nantucket night sky and its usual array of starry constellations, she was certain of her discovery. Confirmed by her father, and recorded at the Harvard College Observatory, the comet was soon spotted and reported by other observers, but Maria's observation prevailed. Maria Mitchell enjoyed the distinction of being the first woman admitted to the American Academy of Arts and Sciences; was bestowed a gold medal by King Frederick of Denmark; was appointed the first professor of astronomy at Vassar, the first women's college in the United States; and was a founder and president of the American Association for the Advancement of Women. Maria Mitchell was certainly one of Nantucket's distinguished citizens. A major contribution was as the Nantucket Atheneum's librarian, its first, for more than twenty years. Her family is widely credited for being among the group of the town's intellectuals who began planning for a larger institution to house the existing library's small collection, of which Lydia Coleman Mitchell, Maria's mother, was the "keeper of the books." Maria Mitchell created the first catalog of the library's books in 1841, a system that would set the course for the library's future.

Housed in a former Universalist church building at the corner of Federal and India Streets, the Nantucket Atheneum was incorporated in 1834. Inspiration for its name derived from the Greek goddess, Athena, goddess of wisdom, an apt title for an institution that celebrates the world of ideas through literature and the written and spoken word. Miss Mitchell was the librarian when disaster struck the town of Nantucket.

On a midsummer's night, in July 1846, fire broke out in a hat shop on Main Street. Flames caught by the wind leapt across rooftops and along the wharves,

Letter from Maria Mitchell to Alexander Starbuck describing him as one of her "Atheneum boys" commends his faithful industry and good penmanship. She also writes of her visit to England and meeting the Astronomer Royal.
August 24, 1859

35

igniting the casks of whale oil stored in warehouses, causing a raging inferno. The Great Fire, as it will always be known, consumed most of the town and waterfront, leaving hundreds homeless and many businesses destroyed. Along with the demise of the whaling industry, the fire extinguished the last embers of Nantucket's glory days.

Determined to rise again, Nantucketers began to rebuild the town. Given the desperate economic times, with so many islanders impoverished, it seems miraculous that those resourceful townspeople could pull together to create what we know today as the town of Nantucket. The Atheneum was one of the buildings reduced to ashes. The new library, designed by architect Frederick Brown Coleman in Greek Revival style, had as its founding principle the Greek goddess's ideals, and became the cultural and educational center of the community.

Photographic portrait of Frederick Douglass

Beginning in the nineteenth century and continuing to this day, the Atheneum has provided a forum for some of our nation's eminent figures, who through lectures given there opened up their world to Nantucket. In 1841, one of the leaders of the abolitionist movement, Frederick Douglass, born in slavery, for the first time spoke to a mixed-race audience at a meeting of the Nantucket Anti-Slavery Society, held at the Atheneum. The burgeoning abolitionist movement found a most eloquent and powerfully persuasive voice in Frederick Douglass. As one participant noted, "Flinty hearts were pierced, and cold ones melted by his eloquence." Throughout the course of his illustrious career, Douglass was to visit Nantucket several times, the last time in August 1885.

A founder of the abolitionist movement and an accomplished orator, Ralph Waldo Emerson, also had his turn at the Atheneum lectern. Considered one of the

Looking up Main Street toward Pacific Bank, with one horse and carriage and early automobiles.

nineteenth century's great thinkers, he was a poet, philosopher, and essayist, chronicling his belief in the transcendental spirit in his writings and speeches. Believing in the ability of man to achieve greater understanding through his own inner divinity, he remarked: "We will walk on our own feet; we will work with our own hands; we will speak our own minds. A nation of men will for the first time exist, because each believes himself inspired by the Divine Soul which also inspires all men." Over the course of ten years, beginning in May of 1847 and ending in October 1857, Emerson came to Nantucket's Atheneum to deliver his thoughtful lectures.

Corner of Whale Street and Old South Wharf

Joining the surge of America's great minds in the nineteenth century and adding to the ranks of speakers who made their way to Nantucket was Henry David Thoreau. A protégé of Emerson, Thoreau further extrapolated ideas of individualism and transcendentalism, becoming a philosopher and writer exploring greater depths of the individual spirit, both in nature and in government. Drawing deeper into the world of nature and feeling a need to experience a simplified life, Thoreau chronicled his move to Walden Pond, where he lived alone in a hut from 1845 to 1847. The topic of his lecture at the Atheneum on December 28, 1854, was "What Shall It Profit a Man If He Gain the Whole World and Lose His Own Soul?"

Pony cart on Main Street, 1890s

The Atheneum welcomed Horace Greeley, the legendary nineteenth-century American newspaper editor, who left his own stamp on the *New York Tribune,* creating one of the most influential newspapers of the time. It was a platform for his own political and social beliefs and promoted support of the new Republican party, as well as being a significant advocate of the antislavery movement.

Yet another figure, born on Nantucket in 1793 into one the founding families, Lucretia Coffin Mott was a leading spokesperson for the antislavery movement and champion of the women's rights movements in America. One of America's first feminists, in 1848 she delivered lectures strongly advocating the abolition of slavery and recommending increased rights for women, including their right to vote and better educational and employment opportunities. A Quaker, she held to her belief that "We too often bind ourselves by authorities rather than by the truth."

Maria Mitchell, by the mid 1850s an acclaimed national figure, also was a guest lecturer at this library that she loved and had devoted herself to for over twenty years. In her work as a librarian and an astronomer, she was a lifelong learner. "Let us buy not such books as people want but books just above their wants and they will reach up to take what is put out for them." Her legacy and memory on island are celebrated and commemorated in the Maria Mitchell Association, established in 1902.

Town Crier Alvin Hull in the middle of Main Street, decorated for the 4th of July, 1895.

Congdon's Pharmacy, 1900s

All photos courtesy of Nantucket Historical Association

Town Today

The financial downturn of the island economy—from the demise of whaling to the Great Fire to the ebbing population caused by diminished prospects as well as the rush to gold and the toll of war—was in some way Nantucket's salvation. The town's impoverishment created the preservation of its history: there was no money to tear down and rebuild and recreate; industry never gained a foothold here, so there are no manufacturing plants or industrial developments. In its enforced idleness, this community of eighteenth- and nineteenth-century architecturally authentic structures remained as it was. More than eight hundred buildings exist today that were built before the Civil War. Brought back to life in the early twentieth century, when tourism brought fresh tides of money and interest, this intact harborside town has a charm all its own.

The island of Nantucket was designated a National Historic Landmark in 1955, and subsequently the town was designated a National Historic District. With vision and foresight, Nantucket created its own template for the future in instituting an organization that would protect and preserve its architectural history: the Nantucket Historic Districts Commission (HDC). Created in 1956, the HDC's mandate is to see that all new buildings and renovations are held to a strict code of standards to ensure the historic town's character.

The past is present today. As one walks along its meanderings streets, the town's charm and authenticity resonate with the history of the past several hundred years.

Unique and singular in America, Nantucket is a town, a county, and an island. But for many of us, it is the place where we feel most at home in the world.

Mimi Beman

A living link, connecting past and present, and continuing the passion for the world of ideas, is one of Maria Mitchell's descendants, Mimi Beman, owner of Mitchell's Book Corner. Descended from the Coffin family, Maria Mitchell was Mimi's great-great-aunt. Mimi summered on Nantucket as a child, but moved to the island full time in 1978 when she inherited the bookstore her parents had created. Considered by many to be one of the pillars of Nantucket, she is a beloved island figure, the literary touchstone for islanders and visitors alike.

The birthplace of Maria Mitchell and her observatory on Vestal Street

Her adventurous spirit lives on in the Maria Mitchell Observatory and Association, today offering a variety of study programs and course work for children and adults.

Nantucket Atheneum

Almost two hundred years after its founding, the Nantucket Atheneum still stands as an enduring symbol of community and as an important repository of cultural and educational activities. Continuing its distinguished speakers programs, the past several years have brought Stephen E. Ambrose, Lisa Norling, Henry Louis Gates Jr., David Halberstam, David McCullough, and Nathaniel Philbrick.

Jared Coffin House

Wealthy islander Jared Coffin, who had made his fortune as a partner in successful whaling ventures, built this house hoping to persuade his wife to find Nantucket an appealing place to live. She had been unhappy with a house he had first built for her on Pleasant Street, now known as Moors End. However, the house on Broad Street was not their answer. Shortly after its construction, the couple moved to Boston, and the house was turned into an inn.

Ted Gurley and Marty Teixeira

Beth Simonsis

Congdon's Pharmacy and Nantucket Pharmacy with their old-fashioned soda fountains and lunch counters, stood side by side for decades and represented a touchstone of small-town life. Congdons' closed its doors at the end of the summer of 2007, thus ending 150 years of service on Main Street, and ending an era on Nantucket.

Allan Bell and Eleanor "Miss Ellie" Ferreira

Ken Knutti

PHARMAC

Soda Fountain *Classics*

Egg Cream

1/2 cup half & half

3 oz. flavored syrup (chocolate, vanilla, strawberry, coffee or cherry syrup)

8 oz. soda water

Hand stir flavored syrup into half & half. Spoon stir while adding up to 8 ounces soda water.

Milkshake

1 cup milk

3 oz. flavored syrup (chocolate, vanilla, strawberry, coffee or cherry syrup)

Use choice of syrup. Blend milk and syrup in blender until slightly thickened (sugar emulsifies in the syrup) Whip to be frothy.

Ham & Pickle Salad Sandwich

A soda fountain classic
1 lb. fresh ground ham
(Buy a 1 lb. block of ham at deli – put in food processor to grind)
1/4 cup sweet pickle relish (drained)
Mayonnaise – to taste
1/4 tsp black pepper

Fold ingredients together using only a little mayonnaise and a little pepper. Serve on white or wheat bread.
Serves 5 – 6 sandwiches

Frappe

1 cup milk

3 oz. flavored syrup (chocolate, vanilla, strawberry, coffee or cherry syrup)

3 scoops ice cream

Use choice of syrup. Blend all ingredients well. For a classic malt, add malt powder. For a New England Classic, use chocolate syrup and vanilla ice cream.

Recipe courtesy of Soda Fountain owner Peter Van Dingstee in Nantucket Pharmacy.

Peter Van Dingstee

Leah Bayer with customers.

Stopping by Aunt Leah's Fudge shop is an island tradition.

Nantucket cranberries are dry harvested especially for use in her award-winning Cranberry Walnut Fudge, as well as the chocolate-covered cranberries.

Manager Anna Gulick

A Centre Street stopping point, Sweet Inspirations handcrafts artisan chocolates, with award-winning recipes, including its trademark native Nantucket Cranberry Creations.

54

Tess Anderson and Kerith Harrison at The Hub

Max Berry and Bill Haddon

Scott Anderson

Michael Molinar

Wendy Hudson and her children, Evelyn and Owen

Owner Wendy Hudson has "loved Bookworks since I was a little kid when I found that magical room in the back. To be the current caretaker means so much to me. Getting the right book into the right hands is life changing. . . . I love this little bookshop."

Mimi Beman

Mitchell's Book Corner has been a cultural landmark and institution on Main Street for forty years. In a move celebrated by the community, Mitchell's has been purchased by island philanthropist Wendy Schmidt and will continue to operate as a bookstore led by experienced booksellers Mary Jennings and Lucretia Voigt. As proprietor Mimi Beman, in summing up her decades of running this beloved shop reminds us, "What's important about Mitchell's is that is has always encouraged and nurtured the romance between Nantucketer's and the world of books."

Lauren Brock of THE TOY BOAT

Robin Bergland of TRILLIUM

Continuing the long tradition of female shopkeepers on Nantucket.

Carol Muehling of PATINA

Janis Aldridge

Becky Peraner, Master Weaver

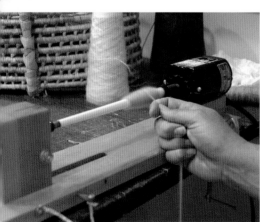

Liz Winship

Mary Beth Serro, Weaver

Nantucket Looms has represented an artistic tradition and has been established as a year-round industry on island for forty years. As owner Liz Winship explains, "Production handweaving, using natural fibers of silk, wool, cashmere, and linen, for the creation of a variety of textile designs, from upholstery fabrics to our signature mohair throws, is our trademark. We also take great pride in representing local artisans, with an eclectic array of one-of-a-kind artistic pieces."

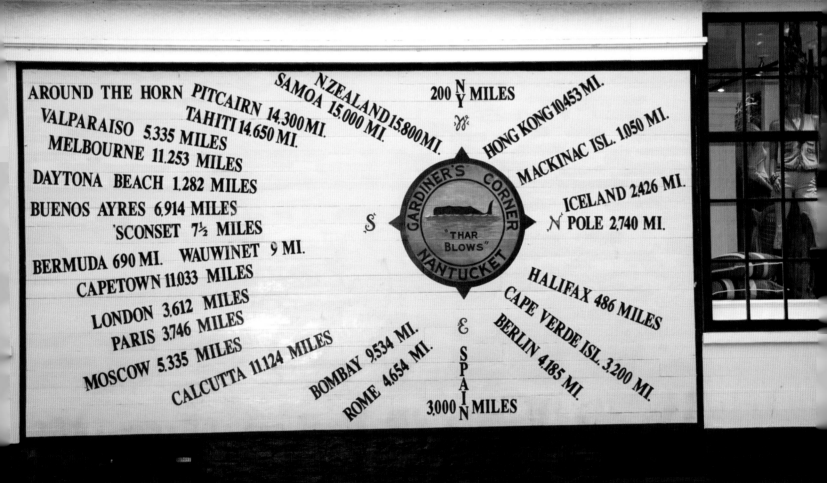

COMPASS ROSE Mural first created in 1936 by H. Marshall Gardiner, is an image based on a longtime nautical symbol, here used to mark Nantucket's place in the world. Restored in 2006 by the joint efforts of the Nantucket Historical Association and Ralph Lauren.

NANTUCKET
1659
ISLAND

Dionis
Siasconset Bike Path
Peter Foulger &
Surfside Bike Path
Whaling Museum
Polpis · Wauwinet
Info Bur · Rest Rooms
Macy · Hadwen &
Oldest House
Old Mill · Old Gaol
Maria Mitchell
Hospital · Airport
Police Station

44

THE CAMERA SHOP

VIDEO
CAMERA

EVEN KEEL
CAFE

eye
of the
needle

Island Pursuit

VIS·A·VIS

BLACK-EYED
SUSAN'S

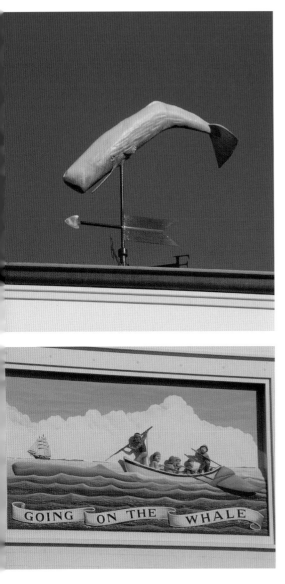

WHALING MUSEUM

GOING ON THE WHALE

Gosnell Hall in NHA Whaling Museum

The Whaling Museum features this 47-foot sperm whale skeleton, as well as a restored 1847 candle factory, with its original whale-oil beam press, a three-story wooden structure that is the only surviving artifact of this type in the world. Multiple displays of historic Nantucket tell this island's story, through exhibits, collections and several films.

Photo courtesy of Jeff Allen and the Natucket Historical Association

The *Nantucket Historical Association* has played a pivotal part in preserving Nantucket's historical heritage, not only in its preservation of photographic and written records of the island and its people, but by the acquisition and maintenance of twenty-three historical sites and buildings that are open to the public.

Charles Rogerson

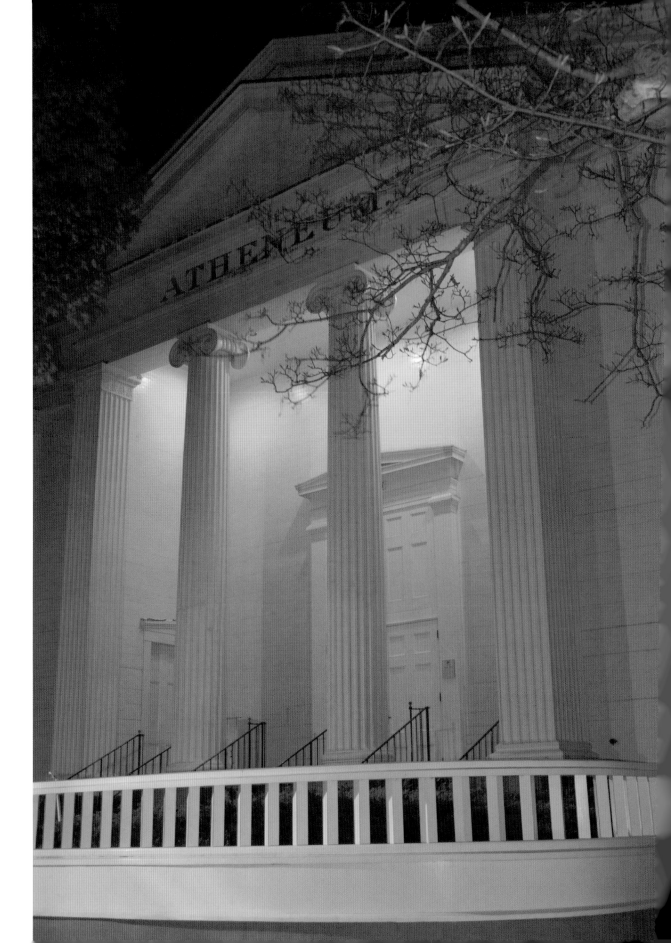

HAND ILLUSTRATED MAP
BY ILLYA KAGAN
CHAPTER THREE

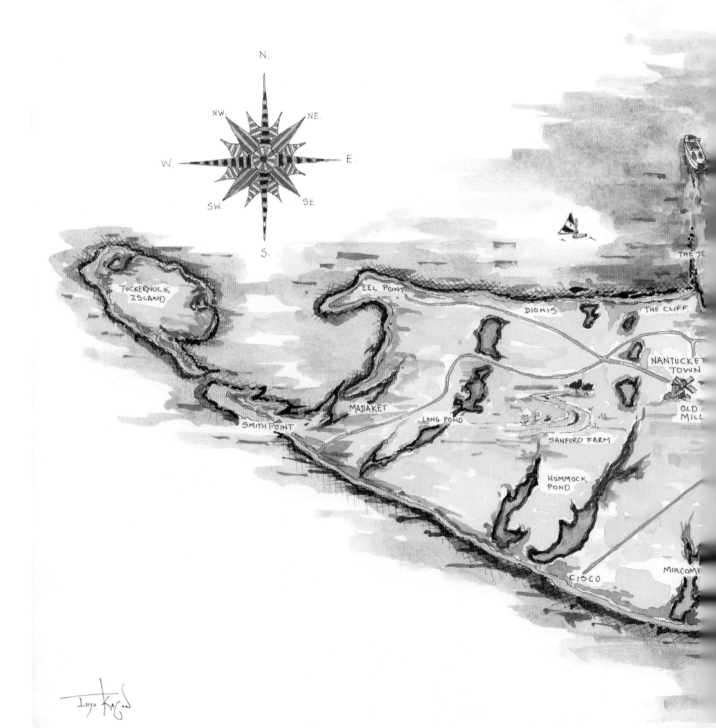

GREAT POINT

NANTUCKET SOUND

ATLANTIC OCEAN

COSCATA

HEAD OF THE
HARBOR

WAUWINET

POCOMO
POINT

QUIDNET

COATUE

POLPIS

SESACHACHA
POND

GRANT POINT

MONOMOY

SANKATY
HEAD

MIDDLE
MOORS

GIBBS POND

NANTUCKET
ISLAND

THE CRANBERRY
BOGGS

SIASCONSET

SURFSIDE

NOBADEER

TOM NEVERS

NANTUCKET ARTIST
Illya Kagan

The illustrated map that Illya has created is a departure from his usual work. Retaining the traditional charm of the compass rose, an ornamental directional marking found on historical maps, his map is a fresh take on the distinctive and familiar contours of Nantucket Island. "The nature of a map is pen and ink, rather than oil, so this project was an opportunity to work, not only in pen and ink, but also watercolor, which is a change from my usual plein air painting."

Painting in the "plein air" tradition, a genre of painting described as modern-day impressionist, essentially means painting outdoors, in the "open air." Illya follows his vision, traveling to beautiful locations and capturing the essence of each locale. "Almost anywhere I go I find things I want to paint. . . . I like to find places that have history to them, working on location you capture more than just the visual, you imbue the painting with the feeling you get when you're on location. My work changes dramatically depending on where I am working." From painting in St. Barth's to the mountains of Colorado to his travels abroad, each location creates an imprint on an artistic sensibility.

His paintings have a distinctive mark of lush, rich colors and always convey an evocative scene, whether it is a corner of town or a sweeping view of the moors at sunset. "This is a place that is inspiring to artistic vision. Nantucket has a painterly aspect. A lot of it is about the sky. We don't have the big trees, so for the most part, you see the horizon all around you. That's part of being on the island; the sky is part of your everyday experience. It's always changing." He adds that, "The moors and the grass plains are unique to Nantucket. The winding roads that lead through the moors are a great subject; it's a great landscape to paint, but also leaves the impression that someone's been there—a human element suggested by the road."

Painting town scenes brings yet another unique perspective: "Nantucket is one of the few amazingly historic towns that is so well preserved. It is a uniquely beautiful place to paint with its cobblestones and historic structures and buildings."

Illya's avocation for the arts comes naturally: his grandfather was a furniture maker turned sculptor, his mother, Erica Wilson, is a highly regarded needlework designer with a collection at the Metropolitan Museum of Art and a shop on Nantucket, as well as work showcased in a range of books and videos; his father, Vladimir Kagan, is one of the twentieth century's pre-eminent modern furniture designers. "Nature or nurture, I certainly grew up with art as a daily routine, watching both my mother and father drawing and painting: my father doing furniture designs and my mother doing sketches for needlepoint designs and then working on the needlepoint. My first job in high school was to paint needlepoint canvases for the store."

Illya's creative vision has taken form in the fluidity and sculptural qualities of both terra cotta and oils. "In college I began sculpting in terra cotta and found the medium to be very fluid and similar to oil paintings: both additive and subtractive." He further explains, "In watercolor, you're always adding your dark; in oil, you add your darks and your lights and you come back and forth until you find your image. In sculpting, in clay, you can both add and remove, as opposed to marble, where you are strictly removing to get to your final image. I find it enjoyable to work in these mediums because the process of finding your image is evident in the finished piece."

This island calls to him, both artistically and emotionally. "Nantucket is a community. Islands have a tendency to form a strong communal bond; everyone knows one another, everyone becomes responsible to one another. People are very supportive of one another."

With his wife, children's author Wendy Rouillard, creator of the Barnaby series of books, and their two young daughters, Nantucket has become the center for their lives. Illya adds simply: "Nantucket is home to me."

ISLAND
Land Itself

Although the sea exerts its pull, it is the land that beckons. Rolling fields; scrubby dunes and plains strewn with wildflowers; heath-filled moors alive with Scotch broom, bayberry, beach plum, holly, and heather cast a spell on islanders and visitors alike. The island comprises fifty square miles, or some thirty-thousand acres.

Nantucket's unique configuration is the result of thousands of years of Earth's geologic evolution, dating to around ten thousand years ago, toward the end of the most recent ice age, when the glaciers melted and caused sea levels to rise and glacial deposits to make their imprint on the earth beneath. Ponds, known as kettle holes, were formed by the deep impression made by the weight of tons of sinking ice. The melting glacial ice left a wake of fine silt, clay, and sand and other organic matter, which eventually formed the island's distinctive peat bogs and salt marshes.

On the southern half of the island, deposits left by the melting ice created what is known today as a sandplain grassland—an open plain similar to the great plains and prairies of the Midwest, but unique in the rare plants and animals that are

supported by this extraordinary ecosystem. The Nantucket Land Bank reports that the combined plains of Nantucket, Tuckernuck, and parts of Martha's Vineyard represent more than ninety percent of the sandplains grasslands in the world. This rare vegetation supports an ecosystem of animal species, including the meadow vole, several species of mouse, and the endangered short-eared owl, as well as providing an ideal environment for numerous endangered plant species. On Nantucket, botanists have identified more than a thousand species and varieties of grasses, mosses, shrubs, trees, and wildflowers, such as sandplain blue-eyed grass, so named for its thin leaves, shaped like blades of grass and carrying six blue-violet petals; the New England blazing star, a tall, spiky plant with bright purplish-pink bristly flowers; and hundreds of other flowering plants.

The sculpting forces of warming glacial waters continued in the central and northern sections of the island, known as the coastal heathlands or "moors," where coarse sand and rocks were left behind. The Nantucket Conservation Foundation informs us that plants surviving in this somewhat barren, sandy soil are the same as some that are found in the sandplain grasslands, but include larger varieties of low-lying shrubs such as black huckleberry, low-bush blueberry, bearberry, bayberry, beach plum, and pasture rose, along with heather and native grasses.

Conservation groups warn that maintenance is critical to support both the grasslands and the heathlands, as both are dependent on conditions created by humans. The island's Native Americans may have burned off vegetation to clear the land for planting, and, later, grazing sheep brought by the English settlers had nibbled away trees and shrubs on large tracts, permitting the low-growing grass and heathland vegetation to thrive. Now, sheep do not graze on these lands and fires do not occur naturally, nor is land being cleared for agricultural purposes. Left to nature, these habitats would be overtaken by scrub oak, pitch pine, and other shrub species that would eradicate this rare landscape. Prescribed burns and deliberate cutting are modern measures that are helping to preserve this habitat.

This space, a world away, seemingly untouched by contemporary times, is preserved, caught and protected from economic tides. Thanks to the efforts of visionary and committed individuals and organizations, more than a third of open space on the island is forever protected from development.

The Nantucket Islands Land Bank, one of those visionary organizations, was conceived in 1983 by Nantucket's Planning and Economic Development Commission (and ratified in a special town meeting in 1984) with the intention of imposing a two-percent tax on all property transactions. The money raised is used to acquire land and real property for public recreational use and conservation. The first such program run by a municipality in the country, the Land Bank has acquired wetlands; moorlands; heathlands; ocean, pond and harbor side property—so far investing over $176-million to protect more than 2,500 acres, with an additional 105 acres subject to conservation restrictions.

Preserving Nantucket's open space as well as its unique character was the mission of the Nantucket Conservation Foundation when it was founded in 1963, and it now holds title to more open land than any other entity on the island. Its flourishing properties are found today throughout the island: on Coatue; at the Sanford

Photo courtesy of Michael Haft

Farm; in the Middle Moors; and at Madaket, Pocomo, Squam, Shawkemo, and Quaise. Its cranberry bogs are cultivated and harvested today much as they were a century ago in a commercial lease agreement that provides income to support its programs.

The Nantucket Land Council, established in 1974 and "organized specifically to engage in the challenges which sometimes are necessary to defend open space," works toward conservation of the environment and land by "planning, protecting, preserving," and by vigilant monitoring of all issues that impact growth and development. Advocating for watchful defense of island resources—groundwater, ponds and harbors, salt marshes, rare species, beaches, dunes, and natural habitats, and land—the Land Council has generated conservation restrictions on more than a thousand acres, protecting and ensuring the unique character of Nantucket's natural resources.

Other entities holding Nantucket land in conservation and preservation are the Trustees of Reservations, the Massachusetts Audubon Society, the Madaket Conservation Land Trust, and the 'Sconset Trust. All but the Nantucket Islands Land Bank are private, membership-supported nonprofit corporations. Invaluable stewards of this land, these organizations and the people behind them have preserved a sense of space and time. Like our ancestors, we walk on timeless earth and hallowed ground.

Romney and Cotswold sheep at Squam Farm playing their part in Nantucket Conservation Foundation's efforts to research the role that sheep grazing might play in the conservation of grasslands and heathlands.

ISLAND
Bartlett's Ocean View Farm

Driving down that long, winding dirt road, surrounded by fields filled with growing things—all manner of vegetables, lettuces, herbs, corn, tomatoes, flowers—these rolling acres beckon.

Welcome to Bartlett's Ocean View Farm, a unique spot on a unique island, where the combination of sea-drenched air, luminous light, and pure Nantucket soil creates a world rooted in the land and farmed by generations of the Bartlett family.

The farm was founded in this fertile, loamy soil by William R. Bartlett in the early 1800s, when agriculture was an important industry on-island. During the1800s there were over a hundred farms on Nantucket. Along with dairy farming, raising sheep for the cultivation of wool became another enterprise. The Bartlett family was to experiment with both. William Bartlett's son Albert and grandson John continued the farming tradition, raising a herd of dairy cows as well as harvesting vegetables and growing hay and grain for feed. But by the beginning of the 1950s, new government regulations made it mandatory for all dairy farms to install

Ray MacVicar and Philip D. Bartlett

Henry Bartlett, 1947

pasteurization plants. Economically, that helped to signal change: John Bartlett decided that it was time to retire, and his son, John Jr., known by family and friends as "June," stepped in to run the farm. June was interested in sheep-raising and brought a flock over on the steamboat—as family lore has it, loose in the hold, not in trucks—and herded them through the streets of town and out to the farm.

In the early 1950s, while June was raising sheep, his young son Phil took an interest in the cultivation of tomatoes. He persuaded his grandmother to allow him to use her front yard to grow his own plants and soon progressed to other vegetables. This interest was to serve him well as, ultimately, sheep-raising proved to have its difficulties. June Bartlett was referred to the country's foremost authority on sheep husbandry, Professor John P. Willman, at Cornell University—a quirky turn of fate, or perhaps destiny, for eight years later Professor Willman's daughter, Dorothy, was to meet, and then marry, Phil Bartlett.

But the flock of sheep had become diseased, and so ended that chapter of farming. By then, growing vegetables had become a small business that Phil and his brother Henry had nurtured. Phil went on to study at Cornell University's College of Agriculture, interrupted by three years of service in the Marine Corps. It was on his return to school that he met and married Dorothy, who had finished undergraduate and graduate work in the field of education, and when Phil had received his degree, he took his bride to the only home he had ever known: Nantucket.

"I always wanted to come back," Phil remembers. "I wanted to continue farming and to work with my father. I was ready to put into practice some of the things

Henry Bartlett, 1953

David DuBois (cousin) and John Bartlett

Photos courtesy of the Bartlett Family

that I had learned at Cornell, and was able to do that and to improve the way that we were raising our crops."

The passionate interest in farming, love for the land, and agricultural education and training ensured that vegetable production would continue to be the mainstay of Ocean View Farm. Phil did return, for a time, to raising cattle, ultimately keeping some seventy head of Black Angus, but by the 1980s it had become clear that the fields were meant solely for growing crops, and the future of the farm was confirmed.

From twenty acres cultivated for vegetable production when Dorothy and Phil Bartlett started out to over a hundred acres today, their range and vision has expanded. Vegetable production spans nearly every season—from the autumn harvest of squashes, pumpkins, potatoes, turnips, and Brussels sprouts; to winter potatoes and kale; to late spring's salad greens and hothouse tomatoes; and early summer's sweet and sugar snap peas and beans; and, finally, to summer's abundance of fresh lettuces and herbs, zucchini and summer squashes, and the ineffable sun-warmed field tomatoes and long-awaited sweet corn. At the peak of the season, the Bartletts harvest four to five acres of tomatoes and more than forty acres of corn.

As their vegetable production increased, it wasn't much of a leap to consider the cultivation of flowers and ornamental plants, a decision that has helped bring the farm into the twenty-first century with wide-ranging business enterprises, a plan for the future, and a new generation of Bartletts growing up on the land.

Dorothy Bartlett

Phil Bartlett

John, David, and Phil Bartlett

More than an acre of modern, climate-controlled, Dutch-designed glass green-houses and some three acres of poly-covered greenhouses provide production space for new plantings and cultivation of vegetables, flowers, and ornamental plants.

Today, Bartlett's Ocean View Farm has grown into an extraordinary commercial enterprise, with a new retail center, selling not only all of their own farm-grown produce but also carrying a broad range of gourmet foods and home and kitchen products and supplies. In addition, the market kitchen has grown into a full-service commercial operation, offering a variety of freshly made entrées and side dishes, condiments, daily soups and sandwiches, and an assortment of desserts.

The next generation is already up and running on this family farm: Phil and Dorothy's four children all play vital roles. Cynthia, who earned a degree in accounting, is the farm's bookkeeper; John, like his father before him, graduated from Cornell with an agricultural degree and is the Ocean View Farm's CEO (along with his wife, Rebecca, also a graduate of Cornell, who is the farm's controller); and twins David and Daniel, field-crops manager and head mechanic, respectively. Dorothy Bartlett considers them fortunate: "My philosophy is that your children will be happy any-where, if they are happy doing the work they do. Turns out, this is what makes them happy." Phil adds, "I'm proud that we've come as far as we have and that the rest of the family is going to carry on the tradition that's been started."

The seventh generation of Bartletts is coming right up. Like the previous gener-ations, these children are breathing the same air, playing in the same earth, watch-ing things grow, and learning to love the land and understand their place in it.

With a visionary nod to future generations, the Bartlett family reached an agreement with the Nantucket Land Council for the preservation of over a hundred acres, a little less than half of their total land holdings, with the provision that the land would remain as agricultural ground, thus preserving Bartlett's Ocean View Farm for all time. As Dorothy reminds us: "Agriculture speaks to a great many people; when we go back to the beginning of what we know of life, it was a life created from the land—always that attachment to the land—everything that grows takes us back to our very roots and forms a strong connection. That's the kind of message a farm evokes, bringing us back to nature."

Cindy Bartlett Bopp, Rebecca Bartlett, and Dorothy Bartlett   *Daniel Bartlett*   *Baby Bartlett*

Bartlett children

If there is one recipe that my family and friends relish every summer that is dependent upon the freshest to-matoes and garden-fresh basil, it is this one. Summer brings many pleasures, but surely one of the simplest is gathering the ingredients, fresh off the vine and out of the ground, and preparing this easy sauce, which my twin sister, Maura, taught me how to make, just as her Swiss husband's aunt taught her. Originating in Milano, Italy, this recipe now finds its way to tables across Europe and America. The preparation couldn't be simpler or faster, and best of all, as it requires no cooking, can be ready and waiting for guests to arrive.

Milanese Pesto

3 – 4 medium-sized tomatoes, blanched for a minute or less just to
loosen the skin, peeled and deseeded

3 – 4 cloves of garlic (as little or as much as one likes)

Large bunch basil

Extra-virgin olive oil

Freshly ground salt and freshly ground pepper

In food processor, pour in olive oil to cover the bottom surface, put in prepared tomatoes and garlic and fill to the top with washed basil leaves. Grind fresh pepper and salt to taste and process by pulsing until you get desired texture, which should be a bit chunky.

We serve this as a sauce over angel hair or spaghettini pasta as a first course, with heaping spoons of freshly grated Parmigiano Reggiano cheese. This pesto is also excellent as an accompaniment to fish or vegetables.

Moors End Farm

When Steve Slosek's father, dairy farmer Stan Slosek, bought this farm on Polpis Road out of bankruptcy in 1958, there were three farms on island. The decision to move their small dairy business from South Attleboro, Massachusetts, was to pave the way for a life change for the next two generations of Sloseks, all of whom have planted themselves here on this same patch of earth and agricultural land.

Steve came over as a boy on the steamer *Nantucket* on the 22nd of December, 1958, and was instantly captivated. That first Christmas, the island was snowed in, and to his amazement he witnessed "these monster iceboats; they were putting ten, twelve, fourteen people in these iceboats. My first impression: people do stuff here." Nantucket's unique character suited this independent young man. But the dairy business was to be a failing enterprise. With new laws that strictly regulated pasteurization and milk coming on-island from large, off-island dairies, times had changed. In 1967, Steve was drafted and served in Vietnam. In 1968, the dairy farm went out of business.

Abby Slosek Wullschleger and Sue Slosek

"I like working with my parents, hearing their stories," reflects Abby. "It makes me glad that my kids are going to be raised in a place where they've be wandering around out in the corn with their grandfather picking corn, hanging out with their grandmother while they sell vegetables, and that's so important to me: that my kids will be close to my parents."

The land lay fallow until after Steve had served in Vietnam. Having trained in air-traffic control, he went on to a stint at the Air Force School in Biloxi, Mississippi, before returning to Nantucket and meeting and marrying Sue. Steve went to work with his father in the trucking business, and Sue planted a small garden, intended only for family use. Tomatoes flourished: "I had more tomatoes than I knew what to do with, so I put them on a little stand to sell. Looked like growing vegetables could be a good idea." That was to be the beginning of a life-sustaining move back to the land. "I didn't know anything," remarks Steve. "I knew more about cars than I knew about vegetables."

But he soon fixed that. He spent two years at the Stockbridge School of Agriculture, a branch of the University of Massachusetts, and began to learn what it took to be a farmer.

"I enjoyed being there; I knew what it was all about, and I was impressed by a lot of the professors; I learned as much as I possibly could in those two years."

Making a living off the land requires an independence of spirit and a hardy soul.

"A lot of people couldn't do it. It's hard work. Farming is a way of life," says Sue Slosek matter of factly. "I am sure that this is what I am meant to be doing. I love the work; probably love it too much," adding with a laugh, "my house shows that I don't love housework, that's for sure."

The daughter of a dairy farmer in Vermont and one of seven in her family, Sue grew up understanding the challenges of a farm, "We all had chores; we all had to work real hard."

Photo by Cary Hazlegrove
Courtesy of the Slosek Family

Hard work is a running theme in this family. It would seem that farming was a life that many people could only imagine, which earns this wry response from daughter, Abby Slosek Wullschleger: "They would dream about it, then at the end of thirty weeks of working seven days a week would think, 'God this is hard work.' It is hard. It's not for everybody."

"Farming is a way of life," adds son, Sam Slosek. "It's not really a lifestyle: there's not a lot of money in it and it's a lot of work. It's easy for us to look past that, but for other people who see us working as hard as we do . . . it's challenging."

The division of labor falls into several categories: Sue and Abby run the nursery business, which started out based on customer demand. "While Steve was planting corn, people would ask for flowers," explains Sue. "I hope you can justify using up this land for flowers," was Steve's taciturn comment. Today, revenue from the annuals and perennials provides Moors End with an important part of their agricultural growth. Sam and Steve take on the responsibilities of the field work—planting and cultivating crops that include tomatoes, cucumbers, lettuce, squash, and five varieties of corn—as well as the maintenance and construction issues that are a daily part of farm life.

Abby and Sam returned to the farm of their own accord. "I think one of the reasons my brother and I did come back here is that my parents never pushed us to come back and be farmers," Abby explains. A graduate in English literature of Tufts University, she taught school before the land and the island, and the pull of family, brought her back. "There's freedom in farming," says Abby. "You make your own

117

Steve Slosek

"I think the ability to actually grow things, to grow food on any sort of a scale, it's a really nice thing. To be able to grow it fresh and good and healthily, using sustainable practices, is rewarding. To get here in the morning, start getting into my tomatoes, it's quiet, peaceful, the air is clean—I can't imagine being anywhere else."

118

Sam Slosek and Daughter Sophia

schedule, you work when you have to. I like the freedom of it, being outdoors and working with my family." For Sam, a graduate of Rensselaer Polytechnic Institute, working in the dot.com world ultimately drew him back, as he recognized that life behind a desk and in front of a computer screen was not his calling. But they were skills that helped usher in a new age at Moors End, bringing updated computer systems into farm practices.

This small family enterprise, with the produce and plants and flowers for sale at the rustic wooden farm stand, seems emblematic of a time gone by. And that has earned the family and the farm not only customer loyalty but also friends. "We have so many really wonderful customers; you don't even think of them as customers, they really are your friends," says Abby. "We've watched our customers' children grow up and it feels like we're a part of everybody's life a little bit. Everybody comes, year after year, children I've watched growing up now are having their children. . . . I'm having a kid. . . . It's a cycle of life, a nice way to live."

Preserving this land is a point of pride for the Slosek family: "I want to say something about open spaces versus houses," says Sue. "We could all be millionaires if we wanted to sell this place, but that's not what we wanted to do." The Sloseks love the land and love what they do. "I love to work. You do it because you love what you do. We're so proud that there aren't thirty houses out there, which there could be." The family entered into an agreement with the Nantucket Land Bank to sell off a portion of the property, to ensure that the land would remain agricultural ground and that the family could continue to live and work the land as Moors End Farm.

A sustaining joy for this tightly knit family is that they are farming—and living lives—together. As Steve says, "The fact that I see my kids every day . . . that I know they are happy and healthy and have every opportunity that could possibly be granted and seeing that come into fruition." Adds Sue, "My greatest joy is working with my family, seeing my kids every day. They've brought a lot to this business." For Sam, it is seeing how different life is for so many others, where geography so often separates and divides families. "I feel a lot closer to my parents."

The continuity of the land and the farm as a living thread that connects generations matters here, as evidenced in Steve Slosek's governing philosophy: "As far as the real estate goes, you don't inherit it from your parents, you borrow it from your children."

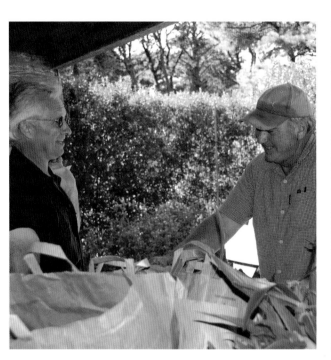

Moors End Farm
Steve's Blueberry Pancakes

2 cups flour (sifted)

2 tablespoons baking powder

Dash salt

3 eggs:

Separate the whites from the yolks

Beat the egg whites

Lightly beat the yolks

1 tablespoon corn oil

2 cups buttermilk

1 cup fresh blueberries (If using frozen, allow to thaw.)

Mix together dry ingredients.

Add half to wet ingredients and gently stir together.

Combine remainder, adding more buttermilk for medium consistency.

Fold in beaten egg whites.

Stir in blueberries.

Ladle onto hot buttered cast-iron frying pan.

Cook over medium heat.

Serve with pure Vermont maple syrup.

Moors End Farm
Sue's Eggplant Casserole

1 large (1 ½ lb) eggplant	½ teaspoon crushed oregano
2 large tomatoes	½ cup dry breadcrumbs
2 eggs beaten	Sprinkle of paprika
2 tablespoons melted butter	2 oz. cheddar cheese
2 to 3 tablespoons chopped onion	¼ cup Parmesan cheese

Peel and slice eggplant into ½ inch slices. Cook by steaming until tender, about 5 minutes or so.

Mash and combine with:

2 eggs beaten	2 to 3 tablespoons chopped onion
2 tablespoons melted butter	½ teaspoon crushed oregano
pinch of pepper	½ cup dry breadcrumbs

Butter shallow 1 ½ quart baking dish. Slice 2 large tomatoes into thin slices. Cover bottom of baking dish with tomatoes. Spoon in eggplant mixture. Cover with sliced tomato.

Grate: 2 oz. cheddar cheese ¼ cup Parmesan cheese and sprinkle over top. Sprinkle with paprika.
Bake at 350° for 45 minutes.

"This recipe is so us," says Abby Slosek Wullschleger.

Prepared by Barbara Harrison

ISLAND
*Milestone & Windswept
Cranberry Bogs*

A traditional New England product, the small, tart, ruby-red cranberry is a visual symbol of the autumn harvest, which harkens back to the history of early America. Cranberries were an important part of the Native American culture, used both as medicine and as food. In the belief that the berries had healing power, poultices were created to cover wounds. To enhance their diet, Indian women created pemmican, a staple that consisted of cooked cranberries pounded together with dried lean meat. The fruit was widely used by the European settlers, and ships sailing from New England usually had a supply of cranberries in the hold to stave off the scourge of scurvy.

Cranberries have always grown wild on Nantucket, but as the whaling industry began its decline in the mid-nineteenth century, several descendants of the original settlers—Coffins, Folgers, Gardners, among them—turned their attention to the cultivation of cranberries on plots of land that each owned, thus creating a new industry.

Tom Larrabee Sr., Bog Manager since 1959

Bogs were created out of swampland at Gibbs Pond, and cultivation of the berries began in earnest under the proprietorship of Richard Burgess, in partnership with Franklin Smith and others, who established the Burgess Cranberry Company in 1905. Subsequently beset by fire and other damage to the crops, the bogs lay fallow for some years until William Makepeace, a prosperous cranberry grower with a company based in Marstons Mills, Massachusetts, became interested in the bogs. The original ten acres grew into an extensive network of cranberry bogs covering over three hundred acres. "The largest bog in the world" is how Makepeace, the "Cranberry King," described the Nantucket property in 1914, when it produced over ten thousand barrels of cranberries. Makepeace invented a toothed wooden scoop, which dramatically increased the productivity of the workers, as berries had previously been picked by hand. Harvesting was further refined with the invention of a metal-toothed scoop called a "Darlington Picker," a mechanized berry picker that plucked the cranberries from the stems by machine.

Cranberry production continued to be an important component of the island economy, especially when Fred B. Maglathlin bought out Burgess and established the Nantucket Cranberry Company, which flourished until World War II, when resources and labor became scarce. In 1959, six islanders formed Nantucket Cranberries, Inc., and bought the dormant cranberry bogs, bringing them back to life by careful cultivation and harvesting. The purchase included 331 acres of bogs, as well as 810 acres of undeveloped land. In 1967, the group sold its interest to three visionary and conservation-minded men—Roy Larson, Arthur Dean, and Walter Beinecke Jr.— who purchased the land, which they then donated to the Nantucket Conservation Foundation. Their intent was to keep the now 250 acres of working cranberry bogs in production, so that any income produced would go toward funding the acquisition of land for the foundation, as well as protecting over a thousand surrounding acres.

The thread from past to present continues with the history of one man: Thomas Larrabee, who first started working in the bogs at age sixteen, was appointed bog manager in 1959, and continues in that capacity today, aided by his son, Tom Jr., who returned to Nantucket after four years in the Marine Corps and fifteen years working in South Carolina. Fifty-seven years spent at the Milestone and Windswept Bogs make Mr. Larrabee a living legend.

When asked the secret or, as Tom Larrabee would say, "the trick," to growing cranberries, his response starts with a chuckle: "Patience . . . and a lot of hard work." With one crop a year, the Larrabees take no chances with the care and maintenance of their cranberries. "So many things can knock your crop out so you don't have any- thing," explains the senior Larrabee. "In the spring, it's frost; on a frosty night it only takes twenty minutes at temperatures below thirty degrees and you don't pick any cranberries that year." Asked how many times that has happened, he replies, "With me, in my fifty-odd years here, I've never lost a crop yet. But where's the wood? I better knock on it," he laughs.

A critical component of the growth cycle is the irrigation system underlying the marshy bog, which protects the crops from frost, irrigates the bog, and applies all pesticides and fertilizers. "It's a very important part of what's going on out there," explains Tom Jr. "We wouldn't have berries without it."

These weathered hands have harvested Nantucket cranberries for decades.

He further details the mechanics of the system: "The first cranberry bogs were built in the early 1900s. They dug out by hand over thirty miles of ditch; there's at least thirty miles of plumbing buried under the bog area here." When the irrigation system is started up, the lines that feed it are pressurized to send water through the system to the 3,500 sprinklers, pumping out millions of gallons of water. The Larrabees are quick to note that "Every bit of water that we put on the bog is going back to the aquifer or into Gibbs Pond or Tom Nevers Pond. It's not wasted water, it's all going back into our own little ecosystem on the island here." The sprinklers are individually screwed into the irrigation pipe, known as the lateral line, which is buried in the bog. The sprinkler heads are installed every spring and picked up again every fall. Intensive manual labor—with help from the migrant farm workers who come to Nantucket in the spring and stay through harvest season—is required to see that each individual sprinkler is twisted on and attached to the line in the spring and then untwisted and stacked every fall, done section by section as each portion of the bog is harvested. The irrigation system, of necessity, is in the first stages of modernization, which will be a five- to ten-year process. Five thousand smaller and more efficient sprinkler heads will replace the existing sprinklers, and will be permanently installed in the plumbing lines, providing greater efficiency of water usage, as well as greater coverage for the misting of fertilization and insecticides.

Tom Larrabee, Jr.

The process of growing and maintaining cranberries is much like any other aspect of farming: work continues throughout the year. As the current year's crops are coming to fruition, usually late in August, the next year's crop, called the terminal bud, is just starting to grow on the vine. September marks the autumn harvest. Harvesting today is done by the wet-picking method, using flails that gently detach the berries from the vines, reducing bruising and damage. In a good year, the Conservation Foundation can anticipate shipping twelve thousand barrels a year, each barrel equaling a hundred pounds of cranberries. Their best year brought thirty thousand barrels, their worst year, nine thousand. The Larrabees book the necessary boat reservations through the Steamship Authority months in advance, as truckloads of harvested cranberries have to make their way to the mainland where they will be processed by Decas Cranberry Products, based in Carver, Massachusetts. "After picking season is over, we let the picking water go back to the pond, and the bogs have a chance to dry out and recover a little bit. All this time, that terminal bud is continuing to form on the vine. In the winter, when things start to get cold, we'll put what they call a winter flood on, cover the vines with water, which will protect the vine itself and the root system from freezing over the winter. The vines go into a dormant stage at that point. In the spring, the terminal bud will really start to form and grow and that will turn into a flower," Tom Jr. explains. Summer is bee season: the Larrabees bring in hundreds of hives from Maine and the bees pollinate the flowering cranberry bud, a wonderful offshoot of which is home-harvested Nantucket Cranberry Honey, sold on island.

By early July, the berry is starting to form—a precious commodity that has been carefully nurtured and protected through this whole process, particularly from the harmful effects of frost. Sweeping sprays of pesticide and fertilizer ensure the growing cranberries are protected from harmful insects and have the nutrients needed for healthy growth. By August, the berry itself is heading into the final stage of maturation, growing plump and red. Within weeks, the cranberries will be harvested, beginning mid-September and finishing by the end of October, when a new cranberry season begins again.

Three generations of Larrabees

On a thirty-seven-acre bog out in Polpis, the Nantucket Conservation Foundation and the Larrabees are engaged in an experiment in organic farming. The Windswept Bog is an organic bog where cranberries are cultivated without the use of traditional fertilizers or insecticides, adhering to the restrictions and principles of organic farming. "A lot of hand-weeding goes on over there to keep the grasses out of the vines," explains Tom Jr. "Pretty labor-intensive; it's the price you pay." The last several years have brought hard-won experience and success. "This year, beneficial insects such as praying mantises and grasshoppers, certain spiders, and birds all contributed to controlling the insects that target the cranberry fruit—such as the black-headed fire worm, which eats the new growth and the bud from the vine, and the cranberry fruit worm, the larvae of which drill into the berry itself and then eat the fruit from the inside out: once inside, the outside of the fruit protects them." Innovative water-management practices have also made a difference in production: "Holding water later into the spring season before we've drained it off has helped to handle the insect problem; the insects we're going after have hatched under water and drowned. The downside of holding water is that the numbers of blooms that flower on the cranberry are lessened. It's a tradeoff: fewer insects, but lower yield. We've done this for several years and now we are able to revert to a more regular draining cycle. Next year, we'll hold water on half of the bog to evaluate. We're looking to find that balance ecologically." Tom continues, "We're not looking to make a profit, we're looking to break even, so we can maintain the property and grow a crop."

Experimenting with different methods is finally producing results: from a low of fifty barrels of cranberries to this year's production of nearly fifteen hundred barrels. All the organic cranberries are harvested and sent to Decas Cranberry Products, along with the traditionally grown cranberries.

ON THE WATER
CHAPTER FIVE

The waters that surround Nantucket Island and flow throughout its harbors and inlets, ponds, streams, and gullies, reach back to its beginnings ten thousand years ago. The ancient coastal plains are a reminder of its past and a harbinger of its future.

The New England coastline, from Maine on downward, reaches the easternmost point of the United States at Nantucket. Surrounded by shoals and shallow waters, Nantucket's topography was formed by the final melting of glacial ice. As the waters subsided, they left debris: a mix of gravel, clay, sand, and sediment; mineral fragments and the fossil remains of ocean life that included oyster and quahog shells layered with conchs, barnacles, and mussels, with the accretion of sand in the complex mix known as "Sankaty Sand." This ancient "terminal moraine" formed the sea floor and the configurations of the island that remain today: the tiny outlying islands of Tuckernuck and Muskeget; the barrier beaches of Coatue, Great Point, Coskata, and the Haulover; the high bluffs at Sankaty Head, Eel Point, Great Point, the northernmost tip of the island—and all the gently rolling hills, valleys, ponds, and heaths contained within those shores.

Nantucket's sandy beaches, from the stormy Atlantic coast to the calmer waters of Nantucket Sound, reflect the topographical history of the island itself. Walk these beaches and it is as if one is standing in time itself. Polished granules of ancient glacial remains, carried by coastal currents, fed by the changing tides, sweeps of sand are carried to form drifts, spits, and sandbars. Gathering force, they form sand dunes and build up beaches only to shift again as the ocean winds and currents take them away.

It is an ever-changing and constantly moving dynamic. The alignment of the sculpting forces of wind, with churning ocean waves and coastal tides, makes its mark most visibly in the spit of sand known as Coatue. This long barrier beach is distinguished by a series of scalloped points, or "cuspate spits," that gracefully define the shoreline. Formed by tidal waves and wind that alternate up and down the coast, these fingers of sand are a favorite stopping point for boaters and beachcombers alike. Strong tidal currents develop in ocean waters due to the gravitational forces of the Moon and the Sun, as the Earth continues its rotation, creating the cycle of daily high and low tides. Twice a month, at full moon and new moon, the Earth, the Sun, and the Moon align, producing what is known as "spring tides" (unrelated to the season), the strongest gravitational attraction, pulling the waters and tides to their highest and lowest points. Tides are lowest during "neap tides," when the Earth, the Sun, and the Moon are perpendicular in their gravitational pull, which occurs during the quarter moon.

Throughout the year, nature's forces batter the island. At their strongest, hurricane-force storms and nor'easters shape both landscape and sea. Buffering the southeast shoreline are the treacherous Nantucket shoals, which writer J. Hector St. Jean de Crèvecoeur, in his *Letters from an American Farmer* (1782), described as "the bulwarks which so powerfully defend this island from the impulse of the mighty ocean, and repel the force of its waves; which, but for the accumulated barriers, would ere now have dissolved its foundations and torn it to pieces."

The Jetties

A century of proposals and planning produced a man-made solution to a problem created by a shoal of sand that plagued all seafaring vessels and, ultimately, contributed to the demise of whaling on Nantucket. Known as the "Nantucket Bar," it was, in fact, two convergent sandbars extending almost a mile wide across the mouth of the harbor. Forming a crescent, this barrier curved from the tip of Eel Point down to the west side of Great Point and ending at the north side of Coatue. At low tide, water level was nine feet at the outer bar and six feet at the inner bar. What became most dangerous for ships in the eighteenth and nineteenth centuries was not just managing to pass over the sandbar, but surviving the sea conditions that were stirred up as a result. Depending on tides and currents and weather conditions, the seas could swell and rise up, so that ships would need to navigate a rising wave only to crash onto the shoals below in shallow water. Entering Nantucket harbor was increasingly perilous, and in 1803 islanders petitioned Congress for help. Stories abounded of whaleships and other vessels being stranded on the bar, sometimes for months. More tragic were the boats that capsized in the surging seas, when lives were lost. New Bedford, with its protected harbor and access to the burgeoning railroads, became the preferred port for the increasingly larger whaleships, which abandoned the port of Nantucket, causing the wharves to fall into disrepair and the beginning of an acute economic depression.

Dredging the channel and numerous proposals for alleviating the conditions failed. Finally, in 1880, one last proposal—specifically the argument that building jetties at the harbor entrance would provide a "Harbor of Refuge"— persuaded Congress to authorize their construction. The theory that led to creating the Jetties is explained by the dynamics of the sea itself. The large volume of water on the ocean's surface builds up tremendous energy, and combined with tidal currents shapes the sea floor. The hope of the engineers was to harness this vast power by constructing a physical barrier, and by dredging a portion of the sea floor, a new, deep channel could be opened through the Bar. They began with the construction of the western jetty, transporting huge granite boulders from a quarry in Connecticut by train and ship and placing them, one by one, on the sea floor. It is reported that islanders made their own small contribution by carting large stones and boulders from Quaise Pasture, Saul's Hills, and other locations to aid in the construction. The process was impeded by the inordinate complications of navigating the shoals upon which the jetty was to be built. It also became evident that for the system to work well, another jetty would have to be built, which would create a greater velocity of water surging between the two walls of stone to create a deeper channel. In a decision that even today provokes controversy, the engineers designed a wider channel, requiring periodic dredging of the harbor in order to be viable. Some fifty years after the first stone was placed, and more than a hundred years since the Army Corps of Engineers made its first proposal, the Jetties were completed.

Published figures of the lengths of the West and East Jetties have been disputed. Nantucket native Maurice Gibbs, a retired naval officer and Commodore of the Wharf Rat Club, after consulting the National Oceanic and Atmospheric Administration (NOAA) navigational charts, measured each—concluding that the West Jetty was 4,500 feet in length and the East Jetty 5,100 feet.

Creating a channel with a low-water depth of twelve feet, the Jetties, along with periodic dredging of the harbor, succeeded in creating conditions that allowed large and small vessels safe passage into Nantucket's harbor. But, as Nantucket historian Edouard Stackpole noted upon their completion, these man-made edifices "stand as monuments to lost opportunity." Too late to save the whaling fleets, the Jetties did serve to create a harbor that not only served as refuge for ships at sea, but now helped to foster the burgeoning tourism trade and created favorable conditions for all those who come to Nantucket by sea, whatever their interests or oc-cupations.

Michael Manville's article in *Nantucket Magazine* (Summer 2000) serves to remind us that "no human con-struction can simply alter the sea. . . ." Citing the late Dr. Wesley Tiffney, former director of the University of Massachusetts Field Station on Nantucket, Manville writes, ". . . The jetties did not simply carve a channel, they also interrupted a pattern of wind and wave movement that had existed for thousands of years. The Nantucket Bar was formed and maintained by northwest winds that drove waves from beyond the Cliff down toward town, carrying with them massive quantities of sand. When the west jetty was built it disrupted this flow. Sand built up outside its wall, and over time hundreds of thousands of tons of it were redirected and deposited."

Sand from the dredging process was deposited inside the harbor and helped to create what is known today as Children's Beach, which was augmented from time to time by sand dredged in the harbor proper. Moving tons of sand created the stretch of shoreline westward: Jetties Beach, the privately owned Cliffside Beach Club, and Steps Beach.

The jarring, jagged face of erosion in 'Sconset.

Photo courtesy Rob Benchley The Nantucket Independent

After decades of watching the shifting shoreline, Maurice Gibbs offers this observation: "When I was a boy, one could park at the Jetties parking lot, open the window, and throw a stone into the water. That edge of the parking lot is now over 150 yards away. But another factor needs to be discussed—the horizontal transport of sand on the wind of winter storms. In my childhood (1930s and '40s), every year the sand dunes that developed at the Jetties Beach and westward around Cliffside Beach were leveled by a team of horses with a sand scoop. As youngsters, we loved to watch this process. But as environmental restrictions arrived, this process became a thing of the past and I would contend that some considerable portion of the filling of the inner harbor basin is a product of wind-driven sand transport. It could be thirty to forty percent of the problem in this area of the harbor."

Today, the island is bound by eighty-two miles of beachfront—from the protected calm waters found in the Harbor and Nantucket Sound, to the strong, sweeping surf of the Atlantic Ocean side of the island. An oasis of nature, sun, sand, and sea combine in transporting beauty.

149

On the seashore at Nantucket, I saw the play of the Atlantic with the coast. Here was wealth; every wave reached a quarter of a mile along shore as it broke. . . . Ah what freedom and grace and beauty with all this might!

Ralph Waldo Emerson, 1847

Standing sentry between land and sea, and providing a powerful visual marker of safety to seafaring vessels, three lighthouses on Nantucket remain today as protectors of mariners and beacons of light.

Brant Point Lighthouse

Brant Point Lighthouse, dating from 1746, was the first to be built on Nantucket and is the second-oldest lighthouse in America; it has always been an important beacon for all mariners entering Nantucket Harbor. The lighthouse that today stands sentry at Brant Point was built in 1901 and is the ninth structure to send its signal to incoming vessels making their way home. In 1746, as the whaling industry gained strength, ship owners and merchants presented a recommendation at Nantucket Town Meeting for a lighthouse to be erected at Brant Point to guide mariners around the point and into the inner harbor. The original structure was destroyed by fire in 1757, and a second wooden lighthouse went down in a late-winter storm in 1774. Over the years, seven lighthouses have been lost to fire, storms, disrepair, or age; the eighth, constructed of brick alongside a brick keeper's house, remained in use until 1900. Today, minus the lantern room at the top, the tower is on the grounds of the U. S. Coast Guard Station Brant Point. The current lighthouse, built in 1901 some six hundred feet from the original site, was refurbished in 2000 and has stood the test of time, continuing to light the way. Rising twenty-six feet on its riprap foundation, its red light flashes its signal every four seconds, and the foghorn, automated in 1965, sounds its blast every ten seconds.

A beacon familiar to boatloads of passengers, Brant Point Lighthouse welcomes both visitors and home-coming islanders, and is acknowledged as an iconic symbol of Nantucket itself. Following a longstanding tradi-tion, as the departing boat rounds Brant Point a passenger tosses a penny overboard, in the hope of returning to the island.

Great Point Lighthouse

Standing at the northernmost tip of the island, originally called Sandy Point, Great Point Lighthouse for more than two centuries has been warning shipping of the hazardous shoals in the waters east and south of Nan-tucket. The first lighthouse was constructed in1785, following an appeal from islanders for a navigational aid in the busy shipping lanes of Nantucket Sound and the Atlantic Ocean. As Nantucket was moving toward its future as an important whaling port, a petition of the island's representative to the Great and General Court of Massachusetts was heard, and Nantucket Light, as the lighthouse was first named, was established. In 1816, the original structure, a simple wooden tower, was destroyed by fire, which some suggested was arson. Peti-tions to Congress for the funds to rebuild were successful, and by the spring of 1818 a new tower was in place, this time constructed of rubble stone and granite. The gleaming, whitewashed tower was sixty feet tall, rising dramatically on this barren outpost and perilously close to the sea. Exposed as it was to the notorious storms that rage periodically over Nantucket, it was almost inevitable that one of those storms would take its toll, and in 1984 a powerful nor'easter brought the tower down and broke through the barrier beach—for a time, turn-ing Great Point into an island. What stands today is a replica of the tower built in 1818. Heeding the petitions of islanders, as well as garnering congressional support, Massachusetts Senator Edward M. Kennedy helped to spearhead efforts to obtain federal money to fund the rebuilding. The new Great Point Light was moved three hundred yards to the west of its previous location and constructed with some of the original 1818 rubble stone. Great Point stands taller, too. At seventy feet, this new tower looms over the horizon beaming its light farther out to sea. Dedicated in 1986, the new light was christened by Senator Kennedy, joined by relatives of the original keepers. Today, Great Point Lighthouse continues to shine as an important navigational tool to mariners and as a beacon of light to all.

Sankaty Head Lighthouse

On the eastern shore of Nantucket, on a ninety-foot bluff known as Sankaty Head, near the village of Siasconset, stands the Sankaty Head Lighthouse. This is the third lighthouse to be erected on the island; again, because of the great need to establish a navigational aid in traversing the dangerous shoals and reefs. In James W. Claflin's series of booklets on Nantucket's lighthouses, he quotes a report by I. W. P. Lewis, a civil engineer contributing to the U. S. Light-House Survey in 1843, speaking to the need for the establishment of this lighthouse: "There is a . . . fatal spot upon the coast of Massachusetts, where many a brave heart and many a gallant ship lie buried in one common grave. The shoals of Nantucket are known and dreaded by every navigator on the Atlantic seaboard. . . . The establishment of a light house at Siasconsett would be more generally useful to the commerce of the United States than any other position on the seaboard." With increased pressure from islanders and mariners, Congress approved the appropriation of funds and work began in 1849. Built of brick, capped with granite, the distinctive tower was painted white with a wide red stripe. The Sankaty Head Lighthouse became the first in the United States to utilize a Fresnel lens, an invention of the French physicist Augustin-Jean Fresnel, consisting of thin panels of glass and a series of mirrors that enabled the light to be brighter and more visible across longer distances. Shining as it did some twenty miles out to sea, it was dubbed the "blazing star" by island fishermen and was considered to be one of the best lights in the country. The greatest threat to Sankaty Head Lighthouse was its location, standing as it did on an increasingly threatened bluff, with every storm eroding the shoreline, bringing the tower perilously close to pitching over the edge. Several shorefront houses in 'Sconset had already been claimed by the sea. In the fall of 2007, massive efforts were undertaken to relocate the lighthouse to safer ground, and it was moved some 450 feet. The hope is that this guiding light will continue to shine for future generations.

Fleet of Coast Guard boats standing ready at Brant Point.
Coast Guard Motto: *Semper Paratus*-Always Ready.

Lighthouse Keepers

In the late 1930s, the Coast Guard was appointed guardian and protector of the nation's lighthouses, responsible for their upkeep and maintenance as well as for governance of buildings and personnel. The key to the success of the program was enlisting the dedicated individuals who manned these solitary outposts. The keeper's job was a lonely one. It required a rare individual with a sturdy disposition, a hardy soul, and a tireless ability to do the hard work it took to keep the light burning bright through every night. By the end of the 1960s, the Coast Guard had automated all three of Nantucket's lighthouses, along with most of the rest of the nation's beacons, thus ending an important maritime trade that had seen countless sailors safely home. The lighthouses continue that tradition today, with electronic foghorns that sound their warning blast in foggy conditions and powerful, automatic, modern optics that steadily guide and light the way.

The Shipwreck & Lifesaving Museum

Writing about lighthouses and their keepers would not present the whole picture of maritime safety without mentioning the heroic efforts of the men assigned to the lifesaving stations situated around the island at Coskata, Madaket, and Surfside. Standing ready to rescue victims of shipwrecks and foundering vessels, these courageous men battled the implacable forces of nature to risk their lives for others. The motto of the nineteenth-century U. S. Life-Saving Service, "You have to go out, but you don't have to come back," embodies the unparalleled heroism of that band of intrepid surfmen. The Shipwreck & Lifesaving Museum was established to tell the story of their extraordinary rescues and as a monument to the history of life-saving in the United States.

"Bug Lights"

In the 1800s, passage over the Nantucket Bar and through the channel into Nantucket Harbor was sufficiently dangerous that two range lights, mounted on small towers and aligned with Brant Point Lighthouse, were installed as aids to navigation. Dubbed "bug lights"—for the light emitted was much like that of lightning bugs against the night—these small lights helped to guide vessels into the channel. Upon completion of the Jetties, which created a safer, deeper channel into the harbor, the bug lights were no longer needed. Decommissioned in 1912, they were purchased by the Gilbreth family and remodeled to create the Nantucket home where the family's adventures were chronicled in the classic tale, *Cheaper by the Dozen.*

"Oh Nantucket by the sea…Where my spirit longs to be."
Lillian Gilbreth

Brant Point Lighthouse

ON THE WATER
Harbormaster

"Someone who is the caretaker, the protector of the town's waters" is the description that harbormaster David Fronzuto offers, but that is the short answer to a complicated question about the governance of the Nantucket Marine and Coastal Resources Department.

Dave Fronzuto has navigated the complex web of interrelationships between the life that takes place on these waters—from the Town Pier and Marina, with summer traffic of up to 3,300 boats; to the daily life of commercial and recreational fishermen; to beach and pond management, with its emphasis on conservation and preservation; to the bureaucratic business of operating a multimillion-dollar budget within town politics and policies.

A retired Coast Guard warrant officer, Fronzuto is equipped for the challenge. Those years left him with the philosophy that "there are two types of people in this world—those who save lives and those who wish they did." This job gives him the opportunity to enhance the lives of those who make their living on the water as well as for those of us for whom the beauty of Nantucket waters is the hold on our hearts.

Harbormaster since 1990, Dave's concerns for Nantucket waters have changed dramatically. "It's all about competing interests: kite boarders; property owners; boat owners; issues of moorings; environmental concerns over eel grass and endangered species; and commercial fishing that includes conch, fluke, lobster, striped bass, and bay and sea scallops."

The compelling pull of the job is his unwavering passion and awareness that "we still have to have this resource protected." As much as the public clamors for additional moorings, Dave vows that he will not "fill every inch of the harbors with moorings, because the eel grass is down there, and if we have eel grass we have scallops, and if we have scallops, we have a winter industry."

Awareness of competing demands and protecting the waters for fishermen reminds David Fronzuto of the island's history: "Nantucket people inherently go back to the sea." Commenting on the state of the waterfront industry today, Fronzuto adds, "There are probably 150 to 200 Nantucketers—the charter-boat people, all the people working in the boatyards (we have eight boatyards, people who do boat repairs); we're supporting what goes on with this life on the water. Fishing and scalloping always were the industry here; now it's house building. But when we stop building houses, I still have to have protected this resource, so the people who want to can come back and fish."

The years of watching over the waters has not diminished his appreciation of the island's beauty: "I am completely in awe of how absolutely beautiful and wonderful it is, even though I see it every day—up harbor . . . Muskeget . . . Tuckernuck."

It's the constantly changing world of wind and water, the ebb and flow of daily tides. "As you've heard, 'time and tide wait for no man.' The shoals are moving with the tide and the wind. It's dynamic. It's just constantly changing."

This love and appreciation for Nantucket's natural beauty has only strengthened his conviction and commitment to making those views available to all. "One of the things we fight so hard for is preserving public access."

Sixteen years on the job have created an environmentalist. Passionate about protecting the ocean waters, ponds, streams, and inlets, but mindful of the human beings who navigate those waters, David Fronzuto offers this closing thought: "If we can help people enjoy themselves and do it safely, there's great solace in that."

David Fronzuto

Ruthie B.

Where once Nantucket's wharves and harbor waters sheltered a small fleet of large ocean-going fishing trawlers, today there is only one: the *Ruthie B.,* the last commercial deep-sea fishing dragger working out of Nantucket.

This massive, 225-ton, 77-foot diesel-powered vessel, designed by fisherman Bill Blount utilizing his degree in engineering and built in his father's shipyard in Rhode Island, the *Ruthie B.* was launched on Nantucket in 1979. When Bill arrived on island several years earlier with his eight-months-pregnant wife, Ruth (hence the boat's name), fishing seemed a natural choice for this devout man of the sea.

Growing up fishing with his father in Atlantic waters off the coast of Rhode Island, he was caught by the sea. When he was only thirteen years old, Bill was put out on a dory for five to six hours a day—a boy alone, catching swordfish. At an early age, he learned the lessons of hard work and patience, but he also found the faith to recognize his calling. "In each man, specifically, God puts a calling to a particular vocation, and I just felt a calling to the sea and to fishing. God put it in my heart."

A prayer before leaving.
Bill Blount and son-in-law, Matt Dixon, who is also a firefighter on island.

The Blounts are a family of faith. It seems biblical: the parable of loaves and fishes, where through the grace of God five loaves of bread and two fish multiplied to feed the five thousand. Bill and Ruth Blount put a similar faith in God to provide for them and their expanding family, which grew to include seven children. "The miraculous thing is that we have always had a roof over our head, clothes on our back, food to share, and in that sense, He has taken those raw ingredients and sustained us, in abundance," Ruth offers. For Bill, fishing seemed the way to do that, and Nantucket exerted its own pull: "Fishing was a way to connect with this island. I felt a draw and a call to this island, from a spiritual standpoint as well. It gave me something in common with the roots of the people who lived here, whose grandparents and great-grandparents were fishermen and originally whalers. Fishing gave me a natural connection with them and with the island." Bill is aware of the hardships he asks his family to endure. "It's a boom and bust lifestyle." Reading old whaling journals found in the Nantucket Historical Association's library gives him some perspective, as their words, coming as they do from a common heritage of a life lived on the water, chronicle a sameness of experience. "It's the politics of a fishing family. The father's gone, the mother has the reins, she has to be the authority; when he comes home, the father picks up the reins and the mother has to relinquish that authority. It's the back and forth."

Much like the whalers' wives of eighteenth-century Nantucketers, Ruth Blount has lived with the hardships and made the adjustments. The life of a fisherman's wife has its own challenges, and the hardest is the reality that you are raising this family alone for much of the time. "I can't go there—to think, well, he's gone five out of seven days a week—I can't think that way. The danger wasn't in Bill's being away but adjusting too fully to it," Ruth explains. "God gave me the grace to be a fisherman's wife." A sense of the presence of God in all things permeates the Blounts' lives, even in explaining how old seamen had navigated the ocean without the technology that assists the modern fisherman today. "God has created an earth that has order. You can figure it out," says Bill. "The old fishermen didn't even have sextants. A lead cup attached to the bottom of a knotted line (the lead line) would be filled with butter; each knot was spaced to represent a fathom (six feet), and as the line was dropped into the ocean, counting the knots enabled them to measure the depth of the water. When the lead weight touched the bottom, bits of the ocean floor would stick to the butter. When the line was retrieved, the captain could tell how deep the water was, and by looking at the color of the sand, or the mud or shells or debris that stuck to the butter, he could literally read the bottom of the sea like a map."

Even with the advent of modern electronics, Bill looks to the sky and the sea for answers: checking wind direction, watching the clouds and what they foretell, and looking at the swells and currents. "I can pretty much tell you what the day will be." Increasingly punishing governmental restrictions, environmental issues, and higher fuel costs have pushed many fishermen out of the water. Bill's not gone yet. "Can be a struggle, you can lose sight of why you did it. It's one of the most dangerous occupations in America; southwest and east of the island lie probably the most treacherous shoals in the world. But I enjoy doing it. I like the hunter-gatherer lifestyle. . . . I guess it takes all kinds to make the world go 'round."

*"I believe there is a sovereign God who is in control.
I am giving Him credit for being who He is."*

God must have been in control on a cold morning in November 2007. Out
scalloping in his 15-foot wooden skiff, Blount was pulled overboard by the
force of a wake, which tipped the dredges on the culling board. Trying to
pull them back, he was entrapped and pulled into the sea. After ten minutes
in frigid water, fellow fisherman Robert McKee rescued him.

"God made fish with certain characteristics. I am using my intelligence. These fish could outswim the net in a minute. They get pooped, drop back inside the net."

The *Ruthie B.* embarks on fishing expeditions that range from one-day trips going five to six miles off Nantucket
to longer deep-sea trips of up to ten days going anywhere from thirty to three hundred miles from Nantucket.

In a cycle that is repeated throughout the course of a fishing day, the net is set out, spooling from the enormous net drum, streaming its way into the sea, casting a web of netting and chains to tow some twenty miles at a time. Trawling the sea bottom, the net scoops up cod and fluke, sea bass, bluefish, haddock, and flounder—along with other groundfish, occasional lobsters and sea anemones, starfish, and frequently rocks and other debris. The net is reeled back in, spilling its haul onto the deck where the catch is quickly sorted. Careful to honor all regulations, the men toss back any fish that do not meet the standard along with whatever is considered to be of no value. The catch is then gutted, bled, cleaned, cut into pieces, and packed in ice to remain fresh when sold at the end of the trip. Processing a catch is time consuming, so it might be almost an hour before the net is cast back out again, to try for another haul.

ON THE WATER
Family Scalloping

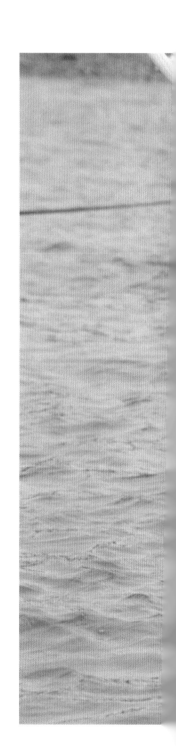

October 1 marks the annual seasonal recurrence of a venerable Nantucket tradition, the opening of "family,"or "recreational," scalloping, as it is known.

The prize is the delectable Nantucket bay scallop, a small morsel of muscle that islanders have been enjoying for generations.

Residents and visitors who want to scallop must first obtain a recreational license from the Marine and Coastal Resources Department. Waders, a pushrake, a net, and a float made from an old tire that holds a bushel basket are all the equipment required. Then wade into the shallow harbor waters in town, Madaket, or Polpis—or in jealously guarded secret spots where the scallops thrive. Hardier, more intrepid souls don wet suits and masks and venture underwater, swimming with the tides, scooping up scallops embedded in eel grass. Recreational scallopers, unlike commercial scallopers, are limited to taking home one bushel of Nantucket bay scallops per week, Wednesday through Sunday, through the end of March.

Laura and Robert Haft

Nicholas Haft and Chris Fuller

Some years are better for recreational scalloping than others, depending on water temperatures and other conditions, especially the health of the eel grass. Most important is taking only those scallops with a growth ring, which indicates its maturity—one that may have reproduced, thus ensuring a viable scallop population. Taking scallops without that identifying ring would ultimately deplete this fragile species, and Nantucket would have lost yet another aspect of its fishing heritage.

Family scalloping is an elemental pleasure—wading in the shallow harbor waters, thick with seaweed and eel grass, plucking scallops up and breathing in the essence of sea and marine life—it is a tangible remembrance of things past.

Nicholas and Michael Haft

ON THE WATER
Commercial Scalloping

Commercial bay scallopers have been plying their trade all along the New England coast since the late 1800s and continue today, although a blight affecting the eelgrass habitat of the bay scallop in the 1930s did have its effect on the Nantucket fishery. A good scallop season (November 1 through March) depends on water temperature and the condition of the beds of eelgrass.

Scallop fisheries in the shallow bay waters from Cape Cod to New Jersey and the islands of Martha's Vineyard and Nantucket, and to some extent those in Long Island Sound, represent the last operational bay scallop fisheries in the world.

Environmental factors exert the primary influence on the life cycle of the scallop, and its fragile existence in a complex ecosystem requires an understanding of just how brief their time is. Their life cycle spans only two years, and a mature scallop breeds only once, in its second summer. Bay scallops are hermaphroditic, each being capable of releasing up to eighteen-million eggs into the water, shortly afterward depositing a similar quantity of sperm that results in a mix called "spat." Successful fertilization might bring about only two fertilized eggs per million. The

Rick Kotalac and Sonny Wood

"Donkey" is the term used to describe the engine that turns the winch used to pull in the heavy dredges, with luck filled with a haul of bay scallops. In "hauling back," as the scallopers have it, the dredge is pulled up over the rail and emptied onto the wooden or fiberglass culling board, where the contents are quickly sorted—everything but mature scallops being thrown back into the sea.

Hank Garnett

Scallop season has run from a high of almost 17,000 bushels in 2007–08 to a low of just 3,860 bushels in 2006–07.

tiny, fragile shellfish are dependent upon clean harbor and estuary waters, free of pesticides, human effluent, and chemical or fuel runoffs that can become endemic in heavily trafficked harbors.

The mitigating factor is the health of the eelgrass beds in which the scallops embed themselves, laying their minuscule seeds—microscopic baby scallops—in this net. Tiny ligaments thread throughout the eelgrass, protecting and buffering the fragile new life against strong tidal currents as well as providing a screen for trapping their nourishment. Scallops are bivalves that move about by opening and closing their hinged shells, which propels them through the water. Some of their natural predators are starfish, crabs, and conch, but their biggest threat is from fishermen.

Responsible fishing will help to avert depletion of the species, and it is critical that seed scallops (those without a growth line) not be fished. Efforts to reseed scallop beds by harvesting seed from Nantucket waters, having them incubated off island, and brought back to the inner harbors, seem to have been effective. But larger environmental issues are at stake. As the Nantucket Harbor and Shellfish Advisory Board reports, the scallop is an indicator species, providing a heads-up on the health of harbor waters. An increasing population and rampant development will take a toll on ocean life—especially on the Nantucket bay scallop.

But hopes are high. After several disappointing years, 2007–2008 exceeded expectations with a final harvest of 16,800 bushels. This scallop season saw 145 commercial licenses issued and a considerable fleet out on the water.

What matters most is what writer Jim Patrick and photographer Rob Benchley, in their superb chronicling of this island pursuit, *Scallop Season*, note:

"This physical distance from mainland soil, and spiritual distance from mainland thinking, has helped bond people of disparate backgrounds into a single term, 'islander,' and has contributed heavily to Nantucket's ability to maintain its scallop fishery as a viable industry and an important cultural heritage. Nantucket's fishery is far more than a business. It is a direct thread to its past."

Charlie Sayle Jr. and David Henry

Commercial scallop season runs from the first of November to the end of March. There are restrictions: no fishing on days when the temperature drops below 28 degrees; the fishery law protects scallops under one year old. Below 28 degrees, when scallops are hauled up onto the dredge board, temperatures are below freezing and present too high a risk that the seed (immature) scallop would freeze and die before being thrown back into the sea. The fishing limit is five bushels per license per day, but each boat may hold two licensed people, which would allow a boat ten bushels per day. A bushel-size box contains about four hundred scallops, making a yield of about eight pounds of shucked bay scallops.

Rick Kotalac

Lisa and Jonathan Holdgate

Experienced scallopers quickly read the harbor floor, letting out up to eight metal dredges that are attached to fifty or sixty feet of line, towing them for twenty to thirty minutes. Knowing when to bring them back is an "acquired knowledge," as native fisherman Rick Kotalac explains. "It's a complicated process. It deals with wind, tides, and depth of water. You know the dredges are full by years of knowledge, knowing the bottom of the bay, knowledge of scalloping." "It's tough, hard work." he adds. Rick would know. An island boy, he came back home from college to fish. His ancestors were some of the original whalers on island in the 1800s.

Evie Sylvia at the entrance to her scallop shanty.

The shucking procedure is an entirely separate, and arduous, operation. Fishermen bring their freshly caught scallops to the shanty where three generations get to work shucking.

"Call ourselves 'sucker shuckers'—we would open everything and anything."
Elliott Sylvia, Irene Garnett, Rene Conrad, Evie Sylvia

Nantucket Bay Scallops

1 pound Nantucket Bay Scallops

6 tablespoons sweet butter

2 tablespoons olive oil

1 teaspoon chopped garlic

¼ cup chopped scallions

¼ cup white wine

¼ cup lime juice

3 tablespoons chopped cilantro

¾ lb. dried angel hair pasta

Cook pasta in pot of salted boiling water. Angel hair pasta takes approx. 6–8 minutes to cool al dente. Drain pasta and reserve ½ cup of pasta water to deglaze the scallop pan. While pasta is cooking, put 3 tablespoons of butter and ½ of the olive oil in preheated sauté pan over medium to high heat. Salt and pepper all the scallops, then sauté ½ of the scallops until caramelized in color, around 6 minutes. Remove them to a platter. Add the remaining butter, olive oil, and scallops and cook as the first batch. Remove them to the platter. Deglaze the hot pan with lime juice and white wine and some of the reserved pasta water, then add the garlic and scallions. Cook down the liquid until reduced by ¼. Add the scallops, stirring until all are heated through. Turn heat off and add the cilantro.

Toss pasta with fresh chopped parsley and lay out on platter. Top with scallops and sauce.
Check for seasoning and sprinkle with more parsley and cilantro.

Recipe provided and prepared by Kendra Lockley, Simply with Style Catering.

Kendra Lockley

196

Island fisherman Matt Herr was for many years the only conch fisherman on Nantucket. Born in Connecticut, he had summered here since he was a boy and moved on-island after college. "Before I knew it, I was fishing—got hooked," Matt recalls. Fashioning a life that is your own is "a very pure way to live." He bought the *Jean Marie* ("bad luck to change a boat's name"), a "downeast" lobster boat, and with it a transferable license to catch conch. That was his beginning. "That's when I started conching in earnest. It was a real struggle. New to this fishery, there was no better teacher than experience." Twelve years later, Herr has figured it out.

The fishing day begins with carting several hundred pounds of bait down to the town pier, rowing out to his scallop boat, and then loading it for transfer to the *Jean Marie*, moored off Monomoy. "Nantucket has few conveniences that a working waterfront would have. There isn't a fishing-oriented infrastructure. There is no icehouse, no bulkhead to load or unload, and limited truck access," explains Matt. "You really have to jump through hoops to get there. This is a waterfront geared toward tourism and pleasure boating, which has the lion's share of access, not commercial fishing."

Joe Dooley

Conch fishing has a nine-month season running from April to December, but intensive fishing happens in only four of those months. Preparation is the key: Matt is perhaps busiest in April—getting the boat ready, preparing the bait, putting gear in order. "That's when you are really trying to prepare: everything you do needs to be geared to those four months. Once the fishing starts you must be ready. I have spent weeks at a time wishing for just one spare day."

For Matt, the process is analogous to football: " You prepare for months to function at a high level for a handful of games. In conching, it is only good, really good, for a relatively short period of time. When it is, you want to haul as many traps as you can. You don't at these times want to be screwing around fixing traps and prepping bait."

Matt fishes primarily in the months that conch are most active. June brings warmer water, and with that increased activity of the whelks (conch) that continues into July and almost ceases in August due to mating cycles. Conch don't eat when they are spawning. By September, spawning is complete and fishing picks up again. October continues as a great month to fish. Those are the four months that conch "go to the pots." In industry jargon, the question is: "How are they crawling? Are they still crawling?" On the move and lured by the bait of horseshoe crabs and other crustaceans, the conch crawl into the pots.

On a good day, Herr can bring in a thousand pounds of conch. "Success is measured in how many traps you can haul in a day. If you streamline a business, haul a few extra traps a day, that makes a difference."

Who's buying the conch? Originally, Matt made the voyage across to Martha's Vineyard, where the fleet of conch fishermen have created an industry and conch would collectively be sold from there. But Matt has now worked out an arrangement with legendary island fisherman and fish-market owner Charlie Sayle to sell all his conch there. Sayle gets the conch right off the boat, packs them up, and ships to another brokerage company. The best market for fresh conch appears to be domestic Chinese settlements where conch appears in a variety of gastronomic specialties.

The years at sea have brought experience and also wisdom. Matt observes, "Operate out of a philosophy of abundance that there will be enough, which is not always easy to do. You hope it works out, and so far it has."

What drives him? "The triumphs are fantastic—the highs are really, really high, the lows are low, but there is always an element of the unknown and there is always the next day. You just might find that next hot spot." The ocean's a mystery. "The pursuit of a sixth sense," is how Matt describes the experience of being out on the water. "You're always aware that it is a work in progress: understanding the ocean . . . like adding a little more color to the painting. I know I heard this somewhere, from someone, but it fits here," says Matt.

"The charm of fishing is that it is the pursuit of what is elusive but attainable . . . an endless set of occasions for hope."

Chuck Butler calls himself the "last lobsterman left on the island" who actually supports himself making a living on the water. A fisherman for thirty years, he started
lobstering when there were seven lobster boats "bigger than mine" on the island;
now, he's the last one left.

"The whole fishing industry used to be a viable thing. But the whole waterfront
is changing. It has changed," explains Butler. "It was hardscrabble until the early
'70s, then became real vibrant, making money until the '80s, then it evaporated.
The waterfront filled up with yachts and turned away from commercial fishing. Many
of the fishermen left the island, couldn't raise a family here on the money you make
fishing, so they all bailed out." He adds, "I feel like a lone ranger." Born in Oklahoma
but raised on the Olympic Peninsula in Washington state, Chuck credits his grandmother with putting saltwater in his blood, "We would go out treading—basically
stepping on flounder and catching them. I liked doing it and I was good at it." After
finishing college and earning a graduate degree in experimental psychology and
physiology at Northwestern University, he followed a friend to Nantucket in 1956 to
dive the *Andrea Doria,* which had sunk off Nantucket. His friend left, but he

Chuck Butler and Greg Bernard

remained. "I'm a survivalist. I had diving gear, started off by raising a guy's sunken lobster boat, which someone else then fished and sank again." Butler raised it again, and went back and retrieved the traps, this time pots filled with lobsters. So the next summer, he set out his own pots. "By just goofing around with lobsters," he had found a trade.

Lobsters are migratory creatures, moving around the ocean floor in search of food and shelter from the predatory fish that feed on them, such as cod, haddock, and bass. As those fisheries have been depleted, the lobster population has grown. Butler fishes five months of the year, but calls the total more like seven months as two of those, April and May, are used for gear work and preparation. "Put eight hundred traps in the water in May, moving them constantly throughout the season to where you think the lobsters are. Fish from Great Point to twenty-five nautical miles offshore . . . all money is made in June, July, August, September, and October, with some coming in as the gear is brought in, in November. Lobsters are purely migratory—that's when they come through." In the past, most lobster regulations have originated from the lobstermen themselves. They set the rules governing the fishery such as marking the minimum and maximum size of caught lobster; not allowing the capture of "eggers," female lobsters carrying eggs; and more important, the development of biodegradable escape panels, so if a pot is lost, a trapped lobster will eventually make its way out. "All ideas we lobstermen thought of and got passed into law to protect this resource."

In recent years, tighter governmental regulation and environmental issues that affect these waters have squeezed the lobstermen out. "Laws seem capricious, created by people who never fished in their life . . . doesn't make sense to anybody who has ever been on the water."

Rueful about the changes on the island and to this way of life, like many fishermen Chuck is facing the possibility of an end to the life he has chosen. The environmental and regulatory issues, as well as economic forces, foreshadow the almost inevitable impossibility of continuing to make a living on the water.

But Butler lobsters on. "The way I was raised, survival by the skin of my teeth, this is fun." Navigating treacherous shoals, stormy seas, and horrific storms all help keep him in the moment. "Can't go wandering off in your head, you have to stay concentrated."

"I get a big charge out of just being out on the water. Favorite aspect of the job isn't making money, but the excitement and exhilaration of being out in the weather and taking what comes from nature. I'm an outdoorsman. Think like a hunter-gatherer. There's something about the challenge of making the best of the situation. There's a whole lot of outright pleasure in being outdoors and bringing in a good catch."

"To find something that you can be successful at, be comfortable at, is a good thing. I found something that I like. Now I'm the last man standing."

Bill Sandole at East Coast Seafood

Charlie Sayle Sr.

209

Dane Dooley and Tom Dunham

Rick Kotalac, native Nantucketer, owner of Brant Point Marine, traces his family back to the nineteenth-century whalers.

Albert Glowacki

Stephen "Spanky" Kania …. leaving the shanty with his catch of shucked scallops.

ON THE WATER
Rod & Reel

In addition to its prominence during the whaling era, Nantucket's waterfront had been a center for commercial fishing—until the surrounding waters became over-fished, tighter regulations were enforced, the wharves were increasingly taken over by tourism, and the fishing fleet moved to other ports. However, the lure of open water created a tradition carried on by many islanders and visitors who now ply rod and reel in fishing for sport—whether surf-casting or fly-fishing from shore, throwing out a line from the wharves, or cruising the fresh- and saltwater ponds.

The more adventurous can charter a fishing boat manned by a captain who will supply all necessary equipment and offer his expertise. Options range from fishing for bluefish in the flats—the shallow waters off Tuckernuck and Muskeget—to tackling white water for striped bass in the rips, an activity requiring an experienced crew. Near the coast the catch could include bluefish, striped bass, or bonita. Offshore, miles from land, the catch might be big fish such as shark and tuna, and the trip might provide dramatic sightings of humpback or northern right whales. The late David Halberstam, a longtime avid fisherman on Nantucket, wrote the foreword to a recently published compilation of some of the best writing on the subject of fishing:

David Halberstam with daughter Julia, landing her first big fish.
Photo courtesy of the Halberstam family

The Gigantic Book of Fishing Stories, edited by Nick Lyons. In it Halberstam wrote: "I am a fisherman and thus a dreamer of a certain quite precise kind, almost always when I am on the water; in my day job I am the most skeptical of men in one of the most skeptical of professions in a world which regrettably holds out fewer and fewer dreams the older I get. . . . I remain forever a dreamer on the water, believing still, often against impressive evidence, that on the last cast of the day I will beget my best strike, and even when that does not happen, that tomorrow will always be better than today."

Captain Tom Mleczko, who runs a fleet of four charter-fishing boats, remembers that fishing was "one of the joys of David's life: sitting on the bow of the boat, in a rip, with the crashing waves, casting the plug, fighting the fish, fighting the boat, fighting the white water—casting a plug into the white water for striped bass—that, for him, was the pinnacle of life—and more times than not, he would catch that fish!"

"On the water, as I am never without dreams,
I am never without hope."

David Halberstam
Foreword to **The Gigantic Book of Fishing Stories**

"The lure of fishing is the challenge of finding the fish, making the right presentation, and getting the fish to bite. And when it all goes right, it just makes me smile. Sure it's nice for me to catch a fish, but it's even better when someone you take out gets a fish on. It gives me a great feeling of satisfaction."

"My hopes are that I can give the clients an enjoyable time on the water. It is to share my enjoyment of what I do and where I do it. The waters surrounding the Island is a great place and when I can share that with people, I hope they find the joy in it, as I do."

Captain Lynne Heyer
with her husband, Captain Jeffrey Heyer
Cross Rip Outfitters, Ltd.

216

Photo courtesy of P.J. Rubin

"My wife calls it an obsession, I call it a passion."
Former teacher Tom Mleczko credits his years of teaching with informing his approach to charter fishing: *"There is a real correlation between the teaching and fishing, because it has a lot to do with teaching and sharing the wonders of Nantucket. It's the study of fish and tides and water and helping folks understand that."*

"The act of fishing becomes as much fun as the act of catching."

"Sportfishing increasingly is about "catch and release." Responsible fishing means taking only what you know you will use, and throwing the rest back."

"What catches you? It's the challenge. Figuring that fish out, appreciating the beauty of your surrounds, whether you're on a river, or a pond, or the ocean . . . enjoy the whole experience. There's always the potential of catching a good fish."

Captain Tom Mleczko
Captain Tom's Fishing Charter

Dan Gault and Pete Kaizer

A commercial fisherman for twenty-five years, Pete Kaizer also runs a salvage operation, cleansing the harbor of the derelict debris and remnants of maritime trash. "The place has been good to us," he offers, in explanation of why he feels compelled to take care of the harbor.

Having learned the tricks of the trade as a commercial fisherman, he is now applying those skills to his charter business, helping people catch their first fish. "We welcome all levels of experience: from total novices who have never caught a fish in their lives to the more experienced fishermen who have caught some of the largest fish in the world."

"Life is short. We're out here to have a good time, so we're going to have some laughs—some at your expense and some at mine. We'll have plenty of action and teach people the way to properly catch fish. The beauty of this is you get to meet all kinds of people. . . . They like the excitement, like catching fish together. Trips take about five hours, we talk about stuff, the world gets small, we find our similarities, share our life stories and adventures. These are the memories that are made."

"The mechanics of catching fish? You gotta believe there's a fish looking at your bait. If you believe there is, you're going to fish . . . you're going to be right there, on top of your game."

Captain Pete Kaizer
The Althea K *Fishing Charter*

"Now as the Dawn flung out her golden robe across the earth."
Homer
The Iliad

What is it about the sea that calls to us, that beckons us home? There is an elemental force in the ebb and flow of tides, in the steady currents that continue on. In that eternal motion, there is peace.

The eighty-two miles of beachfront that encircle Nantucket bring the pleasures of swimming, beachcombing, sunbathing, windsurfing, and surfing along the shore, as well as the joys of being out on the water on a boat, from sailing to powerboats. Town-owned beaches with lifeguards, fronting the calm waters of Nantucket Sound, are on the North Shore at the Jetties and Dionis and on the inner harbor at Children's Beach. On the South Shore and westward, where the pounding surf of the Atlantic Ocean can sometimes be daunting, are Surfside, Cisco, and Miacomet; Madaket Beach is notable for the sunset view, and out east the beach at 'Sconset comes and goes as the northeast storms regularly scour the shoreline.

Beaches that are open to the public, but not guarded, are at Brant Point, just outside the harbor, and Steps Beach on the North Shore to the west; the Francis Street beach is right in town. The South Shore also boasts Nobadeer (great surfing), and eastward is Tom Nevers. More remote beaches are at Pocomo and Coatue.

I must go down to the seas again, for the call of the running tide
Is a wild call and a clear call that may not be denied;
And all I ask is a windy day with the white clouds flying,
And the flung spray and the blown spume, and the sea-gulls crying.

John Masefield
Sea Fever

The sea awoke at midnight from its sleep,
And round the pebbly beaches far and wide
I heard the first wave of the rising tide
Rush onward with uninterrupted sweep;
A voice out of the silence of the deep,
A sound mysteriously multiplied
As of a cataract from the mountain's side,
Or roar of winds upon a wooded steep.
So comes to us at times, from the unknown
And inaccessible solitudes of being,
The rushing of the sea-tides of the soul;
And inspirations, that we deem our own,
Are some divine foreshadowing and foreseeing
Of things beyond our reason or control.

Henry Wadsworth Longfellow
The Sound of the Sea

Steadfast, serene, immovable, the same
Year after year, through all the silent night
Burns on forevermore that quenchless flame,
Shines on that inextinguishable light!

Sail on!" it says, "sail on, ye stately ships!
And with your floating bridge the ocean span;
Be mine to guard this light from all eclipse,
Be yours to bring man nearer unto man!

Henry Wadsworth Longfellow
Two stanzas from The Lighthouse

225

it's always ourselves
we find in the sea.

e.e.cummings
**maggy and milly
and molly and may**

Searching my heart for its true sorrow,
This is the thing I find to be:
That I am weary of words and people,
Sick of the city, wanting the sea.

Edna St. Vincent Millay
Stanza from Exiled

…that serene ocean rolled eastwards from me
a thousand leagues of blue.

Herman Melville
Moby-Dick

My soul is full of longing
For the secret of the sea,
And the heart of the great ocean
Sends a thrilling pulse through me.

Henry Wadsworth Longfellow
The Secret of the Sea

The people along the sand
All turn and look one way.
They turn their back on the land.
They look at the sea all day.

As long as it takes to pass
A ship keeps raising its hull;
The wetter ground like glass
Reflects a standing gull.

The land may vary more;
But wherever the truth may be—
The water comes ashore,
And the people look at the sea.

They cannot look out far.
They cannot look in deep.
But when was that ever a bar
To any watch they keep?

Robert Frost
Neither out Far Nor in Deep

The sea has many voices. . . .

T.S. Eliot
"The Dry Salvages,"
from **Four Quartets**

SCRIMSHANDING

"One of the most fruitful sources of amusement to a whale fisherman, and one which often so engrosses his time and attention as to cause him to neglect his duties, is known as "Scrimshawing". . . the art, if art it be, of manufacturing useful and ornamental articles at sea; and its chief aim is to fight off the dull monotony, which, at times, environs the life of the whaleman."

U. S. Commission of Fish and Fisheries Report, 1887
The Fisheries and Fishery Industries of the United States

The art of scrimshaw developed from the industriousness and Puritan work ethic of the early Nantucket whalemen, who, as J. Hector St. John de Crèvecoeur observed in his *Letters from an American Farmer,* looked on idleness as "the most heinous sin that can be committed in Nantucket." As whaling journeys stretched into voyages of several years, time aboard ship provided the opportunity and the raw material to develop the craft of ivory carving.

Scrimshaw encompasses both the art of painstaking etching on whalebone or ivory and the art of carving with the same materials. In the first, a sketch is laid on the bone or ivory, and the image is carefully etched with a sharpened needle or other tool before rubbing various pigments into the design. The whalemen used sharpened sail

The Marine Mammal Protection Act of 1972 and the Endangered Species Act of 1973, as well as the 1980s ban on the import of elephant ivory, have made the art of scrimshaw more precious. Natural materials used today have been collected prior to those legislative actions.

needles and jackknives, pigments made from squid ink, tobacco "juice" obtained after thorough chewing, various liquids extracted from whatever fruits were aboard—and even blood from captured whales. The images that were commonly drawn were nautical in nature: depictions of a whaling ground, the magnificent three-masted ships with sails towering into the sky, seas dotted with whales and sea life emerging, as well as images of longing—scenes from home and portraits of loved ones.

Dexterous hands also carved a variety of items—from simple objects such as clothespins and other household implements to elaborately engineered, beautifully wrought spool winders and yarn swifts, fanciful pie crimpers, and corset stays. This craft represented the beginning of an important American folk-art tradition, one that is fast becoming a lost art.

On-island today, scrimshaw artists are carrying that legacy forward.

Nancy Chase is considered the "grande dame" of the industry. A Nantucket native, her grandfather, whaling Captain Warren Benson Chase, gave his young granddaughter her first piece of ivory. With that, Nancy carved a relief of a map of Nantucket to be placed on the top of her mother's lightship handbag, made by the master basketmaker José Reyes.

She was given more ivory by William Coffin, who owned a gift shop on Main Street where he sold baskets, and went on to carve a seagull for her own basket and a whale for her sister Susan's basket. That proved to be a pivotal introduction to Mr. Reyes. Impressed by her work, he commissioned Chase to carve three hundred small whales to decorate the lids of his handbags. That led Nancy to establish Cobble Court, the workshop and studio she built in 1960 to begin her new trade.

What has drawn Nancy Chase into this life work is "the challenge. I love what I'm doing. I love making something from nothing. I love taking a hunk of wood or ivory; I love carving, starting from nothing and making something." Chase further explains, "I can pick up a chunk of ivory and see something in it. I just take away what doesn't belong there. I see the possibility of what it might be. That's the fun of it," she adds.

It was Reyes's friend Charlie Sayle who had suggested that an ivory ornament on the baskets' lids might make them more attractive; Sayle was the first islander to carve for Reyes, in 1949, followed by Aletha Macy and ending with Nancy Chase, who carved for Reyes until his death in 1979.

The team at Cobble Court: Tracy Murray, Scott Marks, and Nancy Chase.

Manghis works out of a home workshop/studio, but he maintains a workbench and a collection of scrimshaw at Nina Hellman Antiques on Centre Street.

Scrimshander Charles Manghis was smitten with Nantucket's historical legacy from an early age. Regular visits with his family and his mother's gift of a book on whaling by Edouard Stackpole left a permanent imprint. "A lot of the romance and the history really stuck with me. I went down to Franny's place (Fran Howard's Seven Seas Gift Shop, on Centre Street), and bought whales' teeth for a buck. Took them home and began carving. I copied designs from the books, so they looked like primitive versions of the 1800s scrimshaw.

Manghis credits his mother with creating the foundation for his love of learning and encouraging him to follow his love of art and his chosen art form. "Nantucket is a place where the tradition of American handcraft is extraordinarily important."

Charles uses the resources of the Nantucket Historical Association Research Library and Web site to research the historic images used in his work. "Having those images of the past to be able to draw from gives me the opportunity to create an authentic image."

But it's the history that draws him in, an almost mystical, transcendent communion with the material itself: "Working with the tooth of the sperm whale—it's hard to describe the power and the lure in that. It's big mojo: big magic. When I hold that sperm-whale tooth in my hand I think, where did that animal swim from or to? What was the story behind it? There's a lot of mystery involved in the material, even before I begin working."

Preparation of the surface of the ivory is key to the quality: "Preparation is done by hand and can take hours, working with the material, knowing its limits and limitations. It takes a fair amount of very careful sanding, hand polishing. . . . You can't hurry the process. You cannot risk destroying it by sanding or buffing aggressively. Before I ever cut one line, the piece is sanded and polished to the point that it's like glass. Any scratches will pick up pigment; so by nature, the piece has to be perfect, which takes a level of dedication. Then the engraving process begins, following the sketch that has been made. Sketches and drawings are an important part of the work that is done. Lots of details: historical accuracy and historical details. Nothing is left to chance."

Charles Manghis recognizes the endangered nature of the work he does: "My flip, glib comment is always, 'It's not a dying art, I'm still doing it.'"

"The work itself, by nature, is not a twenty-first-century concept. First of all, importing ivory has been banned since 1972; you can't get the material anymore. The original work was done at a time when the whalemen had time on their hands to do this fine work. It's truly anachronistic to think that here in the twenty-first century one would take so much time, in a period of American history where nobody has any kind of time."

"Scrimshaw cannot be rushed. It's antithetical in so many ways to the way we live today. And yet I am drawn to it and passionately love the work. I love everything about the work and the creative process and being able to express myself through this very traditional art form."

Gracing many homes and carried as an original handcrafted purse, the Nantucket lightship basket is a representation of a time-honored craft that has been honed for well over a century—on island and at sea. Early settlers used a variety of baskets, beginning with those woven by the indigenous population, but the lightship basket has its origins at sea.

The form of the basket may derive from that of the casks, or barrels, created to store oil aboard the whaleships. Hardy, durable, crafted to withstand the battering to which they were subjected, those casks carried the wealth of the whale to shore. In the eighteenth century, coopers (as barrel makers were called) plied their trade in town as well as aboard the whaleships, creating them from slender staves of wood, bound by hoops of iron, with a wooden base—all tightly constructed to hold the valuable oil.

The whaling voyages, coastal commerce, and the transatlantic maritime trade revealed the navigational hazard of the deadly offshore shoals surrounding Nantucket. Sweeping tracts of sand created by the dynamic crosscurrents of wind and

"Making and creating, each time you make a basket I always say there's a little part of me that goes out in each one. It's a circle. It makes a full circle."
Susan Chase Ottison

"The trademark of an Ottison basket? For us, it's the style of the handles we make, and most of our baskets are the cane-stay baskets, which is the typical Reyes style; we followed in that tradition. Rattan is a tough and wiry natural material and is very resilient."
Karl Ottison

sea, combined with dense fog, created what came to be known as "the graveyard of the Atlantic." Thus, an 1843 Congressional investigation, made at the behest of whaling captains, which cited the lives lost and the ships buried in "these treacherous quicksands," succeeded in establishing a lightship station at the shoals as a warning to all seafarers.

Essentially floating lighthouses, lightships were massive utilitarian vessels, outfitted with distinctive lights and an audible warning signal. Serving to warn away all ships from the dangerous shoals, they also were important navigational markers. Vessels could set their courses by the beacon on the lightship, and later by the radio signal. The first lightship, the *Nantucket South Shoal,* was commissioned in 1854, stationed twenty miles southeast of the island. After six months on station, it went down in a storm, blown fifty miles off its mooring, but the crew was rescued. The replacement ship, the *Nantucket New South Shoal No. 1,* served its noble post at sea from 1856 to 1892. It was a lonely life for the men posted on those lightships. Ten men served eight-month tours in that desolate and treacherous zone, enduring isolation and separation from their families and friends for their tour of service.

New England spirit—indeed, Yankee sensibility—might describe the origins of the Nantucket lightship basket. With hours to fill aboard ship, constructive use of the time was clearly explored. Records show that the first incidence of building baskets at sea took place in 1856, when crew members of the *New South Shoal* lightship brought basketmaking materials with them—crafting molds from old masts, using rattan for weaving, and shaping hardwoods for the staves and bottoms.

The Nantucket lightship basket came to be characterized by those wooden bottoms, the distinctive rattan weaving, and the base construction on wooden molds of various sizes and shapes.

The baskets proved popular, originally for utilitarian purposes at home, then increasingly in the shops catering to a growing tourist trade. Thus, a quiet industry was borne—one that continues to this day. After the last South Shoals lightship was decommissioned in 1905, the basket-making tradition continued, albeit greatly reduced in the early twentieth century, its lowest ebb occurring throughout the Great Depression during the 1930s. One well-known Nantucket basketmaker during that time was Clinton Mitchell Ray, known as "Mitchy," whose father and grandfather had served aboard the South Shoal lightship and were notable basketmakers. Another basketmaker from the period was Stephen Gibbs, who was introduced to the craft when as a small boy he was delegated to take supper over to his neighbor, Mitchell Ray.

A "washashore" from the Philippines, José Formoso Reyes brought basketmaking to a new level of appreciation when he began to practice his craft on Nantucket in the 1940s. Mentored by Mitchy Ray, José Reyes created what he called a "Friendship Basket," which took the form of the traditional basket with the addition of a hinged lid. The craftsmanship and history of these baskets is celebrated today in the Nantucket Lightship Basket Museum, which has in its collection some of the finest examples of baskets, from past to present. Displayed in the museum is a significant portion of José Reyes's original workshop, which, for the uninitiated, demonstrates the level and complexity of the work involved.

Nantucket Historical Association
Mitch "Mitchy" Ray in his workshop,
splitting staves for baskets.

Karol Lindquist

Born on Nantucket, Karol Lindquist trained as a weaver before apprenticing with lightship basketmaker Reggie Reed, son of the last lighthouse keeper at Brant Point. A basketmaker for close to thirty years, Lindquist has provided an introduction and instruction on the joys of basketmaking to students for more than twenty years.

Karl and Susan Chase Ottison began making baskets together thirty years ago. Nantucket natives, both have families that go back generations. Susan's father's family descended from the original Coffins.

It is the spirit of American enterprise that created the foundation of a country whose creed celebrated independence and whose vision and determination paved the way for a new generation and a new era.

In an address on "The Young American," delivered in February of 1844, philosopher Ralph Waldo Emerson called out "for America to inspire and express the most expansive and humane spirit; new-born, free, healthful, strong, the land of the laborer, of the democrat, of the philanthropist, of the believer, of the saint, she should speak for the human race. It is the country of the Future . . . it is a country of beginnings, of projects, of designs, and expectations."

And in those beginnings, an entrepreneurial spirit began to take root. The values and virtues of hard work and innovation constitute a uniquely American character that has transformed the landscape of American life. These principles have been at the heart of the individual stories chronicled here, which had, as their beginnings, a life on Nantucket.

Signs on store: HORSES & CARRIAGES TO LET — SMOKE 1815 10 CENT CIGAR — PIPES TOBACCO & CIGARETTES — FRUITS & CIGARS — CHOCOLATES — 1000 Lbs TURKEYS XMAS

Nantucket is driven by an entrepreneurial spirit and a commitment to hard work that lies at the heart of the island.

Nantucket Nectars
From Nantucket Guide

An enterprising spirit and unflagging perseverance are trademarks of businessman Tom Scott, cofounder of the beverage company Nantucket Nectars as well as founder of the television network PLUM TV, broadcasting in several small markets all over the country.

Scott says he has been an "entrepreneur since I was a kid . . . didn't even know what that was, the word wasn't used much then." He was a kid who actively looked for opportunities, selling lemonade from movable stands in the 1970s [gas shortage started in 1973] when long lines formed at gas stations and thirsty customers would be happy to find refreshment while they waited. It's a principle he applied when, as a student at Brown University, he was trying to figure out a way to live and work on Nantucket Island, a place he had come to love.

In 1988, Scott hit on the idea of providing a service for the many boats that were on moorings in Nantucket Harbor. He traded his car for his parents' 21-foot Boston Whaler and created a floating convenience store—along with a successful formula for providing essential service—and called his new enterprise "Allserve." An islander's comment, "Ain't nothin' them boys don't do," became his slogan and described the panoply of services offered: delivery of ice; groceries; newspapers; fresh doughnuts, muffins, and coffee; and services such as laundry, boat cleaning, and waste removal—the last being a pivotal piece of the business plan. Finding a niche by pinpointing waste removal as an essential service, Scott won the trust and the cooperation of Nantucket's maritime community. He had also found a direction for himself.

"When I was a kid, my father used to tell me what I bum I was, because I was. And how he works hard, and he did. And I remember the first summer we had started the business, I think it was July, and I realized I had worked every single day of the summer, from early morning to late night, but I didn't feel like I was making any great sacrifices; I was enjoying myself. So the value of hard work and passion was real and easy." These were lessons he took back to Brown, and after graduation in 1989 he returned to Nantucket with renewed purpose and a larger plan. Hiring his college classmate and good friend Tom First, along with a few others, they enlarged the scope of the operation, opening Allserve as a general store in a tiny space on Straight Wharf and including a salvage-and-rescue operation on the water. By summer's end, with the tourism and boating traffic ebbing, the two Toms knew they had to find a way to stay in business year round. Having scalloped and done odd jobs, they were scrambling for ideas.

Tom Scott and Tom First

One winter's night, at the end of a dinner party, Tom First tried to recreate a concoction made of peach juice that he had enjoyed in Spain. That night, the two young men stumbled upon their next big idea: "The Juice Guys," as they would come to be known, had found their beginnings in what was to become a big success in the beverage business— Nantucket Nectars. The two Toms developed the idea of offering juices in unusual combinations, made with fresh ingredients, and put it all together in an innovative, colorful marketing campaign that used the underside of their trademark purple bottlecaps to disseminate a collection of idiosyncratic Nantucket trivia, which grew to include tidbits of Nantucket history and created a distinctive product.

"We were very much into being as authentic as we could be. We talked for a long time about putting something under the caps, and one of the thoughts was to print remarks or comments about our friends— people no one had ever heard of, but those were the ones that were the most popular. You didn't need to know them. You knew it was real, and I think people liked that." Which is how Tom & Tom, along with their cast of friends (particularly the friend who would get naked and jump off the roof of a building into the harbor) among the bottlecap collectors who threaded their stories along with the juices that were sold.

"Success was defined; it was our definition and we didn't know much, so it didn't take much. It's just that as our recognition of what was possible grew, so did our scope of where this might go and so, too, did our willingness and our desire to get there." In 1993, having been thrown into their own crash course in running a business, they found themselves at a crossing point. *"We were always running out of money, and I didn't know why. They say " buy low, sell high," but that didn't happen (laughs). I didn't know what cash flow was, but we needed money, so we decided to put a business plan together. And we did that by going to the library and reading everything we could about how to make a plan. We were really self- taught. . . . Once again, I didn't know there was another way. I just thought that's what you do, you go to the library. We worked hard."* Coming to the rescue was an investor who came in on the strength of the relationship that had been established

when Allserve cleaned his boat, anchored at Straight Wharf, along with the business proposal that Scott and First sent to him. Michael Egan, owner of Alamo Rent A Car, became the sole outside financial investor, which allowed Nantucket Nectars to finally find its footing and create a nationwide launch of a unique product formula. What started at a kitchen table with a blender and an idea turned into a multimillion-dollar company that was sold to Cadbury Schweppes in 2002.

Any advice Tom Scott might offer to a young, budding entrepreneur?

"I think that if you just follow what draws you— funwise—you'll find it. Because remember: I found this through boats; I liked boats, not juice. But you get lucky being passionate. I just don't think you get lucky sitting on a couch. Your heart knows where to go better than your brain. That's the thing I always tell people. I think people think that's trite, that I'm being simplistic and idealistic. I don't think I am. I think it's the best advice I can give."

Tom & Tom

Photo courtesy of the Scott Family

Frenchie Doucette, Kate Brosnan, and Tom Scott

And Tom Scott has taken his own advice into his next venture: PLUM TV, a concept he believes has the potential to "create a communication platform that is open and honest. And it's not about us being honest, it's about creating a platform and letting the people themselves be open and honest." Scott came to Nantucket television as an investor in a station that he ended up buying and turning into this new idea.

"One of the inspirations for PLUM is that this is such an interesting cross-section of interesting people. I knew Nantucket was a special place, kind of a crossroads of locals and visitors, and I thought, why not? Be a part of something."

Nantucket was the first in what has become a network of eight television stations and Web sites in Aspen, the Hamptons, Martha's Vineyard, Miami Beach, Sun Valley, Telluride, and Vail, with an audience of over sixteen million. Starting with the catalyst of a concentration of some of the leaders in the fields of architecture, business, literature, politics, and the arts and media who visit or have homes in those markets, and addressing the interests of the core communities in each area, PLUM TV aims to make its mark by celebrating and showcasing the best of both. Within that model, there is a social imprint that matters:

"I really hope that the community is able to stay true. Or we're able to stay true to the community."

A third-generation Nantucketer, Chris Glowacki was launched into the field of television by the very premise of the network he has now helped found: the confluence of connection born of circumstance.

"One of the things about growing up on Nantucket is that it is a tremendous, unbelievable resource. A kid growing up here has exposure to so many things you don't get in other small towns or even big cities, because of the intensity of the kinds of people that come here. It's just a great place to meet people and learn about the world and learn about opportunities."

One of the opportunities came in the person of former executive Bob Wright, who was CEO of NBC at the time and a summer resident of Nantucket. Wright provided Chris's introduction to NBC, where he spent ten years, ultimately narrowing his interests to business development through the emergent cable and Internet possibilities.

"I was focused on the notion of opportunities in local media and I heard through the grapevine that my

old friend from Nantucket, Tom Scott, had bought a television channel on the island. We started talking about what that could mean. We had a really good feel for places like Nantucket and the intensity of emotion that people have about being here. We also knew how much interesting content you get out of a place like this. In addition to the natural beauty, there are the people: the visitors and the locals. The summer visitors tend to be very interesting, accomplished, intense people, but to live here you have to make a lot of sacrifices, so the locals themselves, many of them, tend to be intense characters as well. And so you've got a great mix of place, people, and activities that led to this notion that we could find similar communities and put together a network of media properties connecting them."

PLUM TV is now a network of eight stations linking this same idea: that of affluent resort communities with a base of an authentic town or community that is the bedrock of each sense of place.

"For me, it's great to have started a company here, because it's always like coming home. Nantucket is a great test market for us. I have very deep relationships here, still have my family here, and really consider it home. As we develop ideas for things we might want to do across the rest of the company, this is where it tends to start, because this is where we can know really quickly whether it makes sense for the community and whether it's working. I think it would have been very difficult to do this without already having a very deep understanding of a market like this."

The PLUM method of television is:

"To not think about the stereotype of a TV person, to not be scripted, and to be truly interested to what a person has to say. So many people switch into someone else when they get in front of a camera. We make an effort at Plum to try to put people at ease and keep them from switching into someone else. Part of what allows us to do that is the places we are in.. You take corporate CEOs, people who should be completely comfortable in their own skin; you put them in a booth in New York City, you turn those lights on, and they

turn into corporate mouthpieces. You put them here at the Ropewalk, in a polo shirt, with a cup of coffee from Provisions, and you actually meet a human being. That's very much what we think differentiates the experience. There is something about people watching PLUM, they sort of can't take their eyes off it. There's something very different going on, and I think it's just truly reality television."

Chris Glowacki's roots run deep and are now attached to a vehicle that he hopes makes a difference to his island home:

"The mission statement of the company starts with being sensitive to the community, and we do think we play a role. This whole notion comes from a place of optimism, a place of celebrating the spirit of the island. There is nothing cynical about what we do here at PLUM, and I think that does serve to make some conversations happen out in the open and some things to happen that have a positive impact. We clearly have an impact on the not-for-profits and the events that go on here, and on the art community. In a lot of ways, we help to shine a light on what's best, and I think that does help."

What does he hope to accomplish?

"Celebrating the spirit of the community, certainly. And being about what makes this place special, which isn't the stereotype image of a resort, it really is something much deeper. It is that there is a real community. We find that what attracts people to this place is not the gloss of a glitzy resort; although the fact that it has all that infrastructure certainly helps, but it is that there is a real spirit of community."

THE MORNING NOON & NIGHT SHOW
WEATHER 69/57°
* THE LIST   SANDCASTLES
* TERRY POMMETT PHOTOGRAPHER
* WENDY ROUILLARD AUTHOR
* NIC JUDSON EXEC DIRECTOR NCS
* MAURY PEOPLE BEACH PLUM

JAMEY BENNETT
LIGHTWEDGE

Innovation is a key word for Nantucket businessman Jamey Bennett, founder and CEO of LightWedge, a pioneering company that found a way to harness the power of LED technology in book lights and magnification products.

It all started with a high school passion for playing with light:

"(Laughs) It's not a very glamorous story: in high school I collected beer cans and beer signs. I had a Miller Lite beer sign that was a piece of acrylic with a logo etched in it, lit from the edge. Wherever the logo was etched in the acrylic, it interrupted the light and caused the logo to glow. I looked at it and somehow got the idea that if I cut a piece of acrylic on a very acute angle, I could get light to come out the entire facet that I created. And so I found some acrylic, I cut it and polished it, put a light on it, and it worked. It worked great. I didn't have a grip at that point on how I might pursue commercializing it, so I stuck it in a drawer and forgot about it for a while."

In the meantime, having graduated from Bucknell University, Bennett had another interesting idea: harness the power of the Internet to find an innovative way of allowing businesses to connect, and he launched BookWire in 1994.

One of the first business-to-business Web sites, BookWire was designed to help book publishers and printers work more effectively together, and in the process BookWire became an online clearinghouse for information about the business of book publishing. Bennett sold the company to Reed Business Information, and, joining their management team, went on to create several other B2B Web businesses around Reed's entertainment trade magazines.

With his expertise and proven success in the burgeoning world of the Internet, Bennett saw another opening in a different field: the consumer lending business. In 1996, he cofounded LendingTree.com, an online loan marketplace where consumers could describe their borrowing needs and have lenders compete for their business. LendingTree found its niche in the market, and by 2000 was a nationally recognized and publicly traded company, with billions of dollars of loans closed per quarter.

Leaving LendingTree, now with financial resources to explore new ideas, he returned to an old one: tinkering with that concept of the play of light on a page.

"I have always been attracted to gadgets (I worked at Brookstone when I was in high school) and I have always just liked the idea of making and selling things—objects, things you can put your hands on. Lending-Tree was a terrific experience, really fun, and selling financial products was fine, but there is a different sense of satisfaction that comes from the process of designing a physical product, putting it in a package, seeing it on retail shelves, and knowing people are buying it, using it, and enjoying it."

Bennett built a new prototype and hired a design firm to make conceptual drawings of the finished product. Armed with his rough prototype and a few drawings, he called in a contact he had from his previous book business—a Barnes & Noble executive—and scheduled his first sales call:

"I walked in and had him lower the shades in his office and turn off the lights. He said this was crazy, never had anyone come in and turn off the lights before. I flipped the switch and he said, "Wow, that is really something." At that point, it looked like Frankenstein's monster. It was just a hunk of plastic with a handmade aluminum housing on it, but I did bring some boards from the design company. I showed him the drawings of the product and the packaging concepts. He called in the buyers, said this is great, you've got to look at this, come see this, and that was really all the validation I needed. Essentially, they said, yes, when you've made this, we'll figure out how to give it a shot."

"That was in September 2001, and we were shipping product by June 2002." It has been a solid seller at Barnes & Noble since then. Knowing he had a customer—actually two, as Bennett also knew that Levenger, a catalog company, would be interested—he got to work:

"I took my concept, which was very clunky and was really just a concept, and worked very closely with an industrial designer to get the shape right, to get the function right, to get the light distribution right. There was a lot of engineering and development; in fact, the designer did so much work on the product, his name is also on the design patent."

After establishing manufacturing and starting full production, Bennett introduced LightWedge to the marketplace, where it quickly found its niche. Bennett gives his wife and partner, Debbie Bennett, credit for being an "instrumental part of the business. She is responsible for selling some of the largest accounts we have and making sure those relationships stay very, very good. She does a fantastic job."

As parents of four children, the Bennetts did have to face one life-defining decision: where they would live and headquarter this emerging business. Having summered on island and growing to love Nantucket, they took a chance, moving to their cottage in Madaket.

"Pretty fantastic decision. We thought, well, this could be nine months, a year, year and a half, we'll see where this goes, what happens, but the more we got integrated into the year-round community the more we liked it—the more we just fell in love with everything—and we had loved summer here. The year-round community is terrific and getting bigger with more texture to it, more diversity to it all the time."

The only difficulty in basing a business on Nantucket is the inevitable travel:

"Think of it as the travel tax. Cape Air adds a little bit of expense and extra time. If I absolutely have to be somewhere tomorrow, I have to leave here today, there's no question about it. Adds complexity. If that's the price you pay for living in paradise, it's not so bad. That's the way we look at it."

A unique enterprise is quite literally brewing on Bartlett Farm Road. A mini conglomerate of businesses, linked by the idea of fermentation and distillation, has been created under the names of Cisco Brewers, Nantucket Vineyard, and Triple Eight Distillery. For the five partners behind these businesses, finding their way to making a life on Nantucket is a dream that has been made real.

A link to the land and to an ancestral past was the calling for Wendy and Randy Hudson as they each found their way to Nantucket. Wendy, who had grown up sailing to the island with her grandparents and had spent summers working here in her college years, loved Nantucket enough to come back after graduation. A philosophy major, she counts the time spent working at Bartlett's Farm as giving her an appreciation for the kind of life made from working the land and an admiration for the dynamics of the Bartlett family, who had created this enterprise. In examining "what a good life to live would be," Hudson was also spending "all my time at Bookworks," a small, independent bookstore on Broad Street. For Randy, it was his grandparents' passion for genealogy, which revealed that their family descended from the Swain family, a father and son who, in the 1600s, were two of the original settlers of Nantucket. "I felt like I was letting my grandparents live that dream through me, because they really wanted to investigate and learn more about their family heritage. They never got a chance, so I did it for them." He moved to the island in 1988, following a friend from his graduate horticulture program who was running a landscape and design business. He started working in landscaping and, needing another job, found his way to Something Natural, the bakery and sandwich shop, renowned for its artisanal bread. Something of a baker himself, Randy had always had an interest in the food business. Wendy and Randy met at this juncture. Wendy, who had spent time in Palo Alto, California, which was a "hotbed for microbrewing at the time"—beer, that is—had become something of a home-brewer herself, and had brought that knowledge with her to Nantucket. "I met Randy and I just knew he would love to brew beer. He's a great cook, he knew about grain and yeast. The first present I ever bought him was a home-brewing kit. He took that ball and ran."

Left to right:
Randy Hudson, Wendy Hudson, Dean Long, Melissa Long, Jay Harmon

Photo courtesy of Terry Pommett.

Photo courtesy of Terry Pommett.

All of the products are produced on island. The vodkas are triple-distilled from high-quality, organically grown grain and corn blended with pure Nantucket water drawn from well #888. The flavored vodkas use fresh, hand-peeled oranges. The cranberry vodka is made with freshly harvested Nantucket cranberries from the Windswept organic bog.

As Randy explains: *"Because of my background in scratch baking, I was more interested in finding out what made the beer what it was—where did it come from? Most people start out buying kits, (cans of syrup, or dried malt extract); in essence, part of the beer has been made for you already. I was more interested in using the grains myself to make my own. So I delved into it . . . obsessively. It is magical. You do what you can to produce something to ferment, and then you are employing these little microorganisms to do your work there—the magical changing of sugars to alcohol—that alchemy.*

The process of making beer is one where you are just basically extracting fermentable sugar from grains. Grains are starch, which is all long-chain sugars; you want to make those available for yeast—the science of it is employing enzymes in the grain naturally to break down those starches into fermentable sugars. The art of it is combining those different sugars and hopping them (which is essentially bittering the beer with the hops), which is a balance of flavors: sweet malt flavors, bitter hops (hops is a flower, it grows on a vine), and different yeast profiles (there are hundreds of yeasts and they all make different flavor profiles). Combine those three elements and you have an infinite range of flavors you can achieve; that's the art. It's just magical."

Randy and Wendy met Dean and Melissa Long, who had started a winery on several acres of rural land on the island's south shore, on Bartlett Farm Road. Dean, a classics major, had wanted to make wine using island-grown grapes—an experiment that was not entirely successful. Importing grapes from regions in California, New York, and other areas, Nantucket Vineyard found a formula that worked. For Dean and Melissa, who had met while working at Bartlett's Farm (as Dean quips, "Everything's related around here, whether you like it or not."), creating a business out of growing was the right fit for them.

"I was a farmer for ninety percent of my life. I worked on dairy farms as a kid, and worked on vegetable farms here. Bartlett's lent us the land; I got started in this to grow the grapes. I like making stuff. If it ferments, you want to try and make it, as an old friend of mine said: "It's an interesting pursuit to try and make stuff yourself."

What began as a personal relationship—the Longs leased a loft in their building to the Hudsons—turned to a burgeoning business interest. Using a portion of loaned land as well, Wendy and Randy created a makeshift brewery on the property.

As Wendy told it: *"We started with one recipe; from then on, Randy was grinding his own grain in our pasta machine. He was just so good at it, and at that point we were living in the winery and home-brewing. In 1992, there was no brewery on Nantucket, but it was growing everywhere else in the country, so we just did it. We didn't get the fancy copper pots, we just did it the Yankee way with Dean and Randy adapting things to their needs and finding used equipment . . . and that's how we hung in there all this time. Sold our first beer in 1995—that's the year we got married, and that's the year I started working at Bookworks."*

It was to be a pivotal year and a pivotal turn for the couple. Cisco Brewers, makeshift as it was, had its beginnings; and Wendy found herself in the world of books, as a staffer at Bookworks.

The business took the next step with the arrival of Jay Harman, who having written a senior thesis on microbrewers had come to Nantucket hoping to open up his own small brewing business. After getting to know the operation at Cisco, he joined the Hudsons' brewery. He quickly became an invaluable member of the team and a full partner in this growing enterprise.

"I landed on Nantucket, having chased my high school girlfriend (who is now my wife) here, as her family had a restaurant and I could work there. I pitched myself to Randy and Wendy that once I was out of school, I wanted to move to Nantucket and partner with them. At that point, the brewery was still brewing outside, just a little shack in the back. I jumped in with both feet. From the get go, I was always interested in the sales and market direction and that's what my senior thesis was about: the trend of craft-brewed beers and how they were becoming the new hot thing in the beer industry. Today, I consider myself the sales and marketing element. I piece together what they produce and present the story to the public."

Dean's taking the long view of fermentation and distillation was sparked by a movement in California, that of small microbreweries moving into distillation of liquor, so he applied for a liquor-manufacturing license. It was a natural progression and one that Dean, Randy, and Jay could envision. And that was the start of the partnership, utilizing their combined skills, talents, and equipment to launch this new enterprise.

As its daunting first task, the company took on the idea of creating a single-malt whisky they called "The Notch," as in "Not Scotch." (The term "Scotch" is applied only to whisky aged and distilled in Scotland.) The partners also had to take the long view with potential business plans, as this was one product that would require time. Aging is a process and an art. Beginning with the distilled liquid, the journey begins with years spent "in the wood," first in American white oak casks, then transferred for its final months to French oak, wine-soaked casks, which imbue the product with its distinctive taste and aroma. It is a uniquely organic liquid, as the product is the end result of every step of the process.

Jay Harmon explains: "*The unique process of making The Notch—Nantucket single-malt whisky—is that all three businesses have combined their efforts to produce a product like no other in the world. The brewery develops the whisky wash by producing a young beer without the hops; after seventy-two hours of fermentation in the beer tanks, the wash is transferred to the distillery where the alcohol is heated in a copper-pot still. In the next step the water and impurities are removed, leaving a crystal-clear distillate reminiscent of moonshine but barley based instead of corn based. . . . The heart, or center cut, of this distillate is measured and racked into ex-bourbon barrels and then laid to rest in the bonded warehouse for five years. After sampling the wares, the whisky is then transferred into French oak in which the winery has aged its products. This finishing step is a way to add complexity and roundness to the whisky, imparting some additional fine oak and wine flavors unlike any other whisky. When the whisky is ready to be bottled, it will be marketed only at the distillery. What is unique about all of our products is that it is so hand-done, and watched over by just a few people. This is not a factory, with thousands of gallons of stuff, and hundreds of people working*

Dean: "We've dedicated ourselves to trying to make things from scratch. That's what makes our products different."

assembly lines. A combination of hard work and years of skill and patience go into every bottle until it is ready to be shared with the world. To mark this pride-honored labor of love, the label on the back of the bottles describes the long haul that the brewer, vintner, and distiller took to produce The Notch:"

*Milling the grist and fermenting the mash, Hudson feeds Long with his alcohol stash.
Beginning to boil, the wash starts to drip, just think a few years and it's ready to sip.
Into the wood, the whisky will sit till Harman asks Long if it's ready to ship.
Raise up your glass and toast to the skill, 3 men from Nantucket who tend to the still.
Harman, Hudson & Long – bring you, "The Notch" Nantucket single-malt whisky.*

Initial tasting reports have been overwhelmingly positive. Triple Eight's consultant from Scotland, as well as manufacturers of equipment in Scotland, have given Nantucket's Notch high marks for its taste and quality.

In the meantime, having a business to support, the partners turned to a product that could begin production and sales with a shorter timetable: the creation of a hand-crafted vodka. Their Triple Eight vodka, produced from organically grown corn, and triple-distilled from pure, sand-filtered Nantucket water, has yielded a distinctive product offering a range of flavors. Venturing into other spirits, Triple Eight has spawned Gale Force Gin and Hurricane Rum. This is a company built on creativity and hard work. "We all wear about fifty hats, " explains Jay. "As entrepreneurs, you have to do that. Some days we're labeling on the label machine, some days we're mashing out, some days we're out tasting. We're a small company and, fortunately, we're very flexible; we're able to do this." A shared vision for what matters is what keeps them here. As Jay reflects, "We all have the same goal: to create something we're passionate about and to be able to continue to live here. Everything about the island is why we want to be here. It is really about the heart and soul of Nantucket."

Nantucket carries a tide of human experience forward—a sweep of history that informs its present and fore-shadows its future.

Much as the eighteenth and nineteenth centuries' vibrant whaling industry brought together a vast cultural mix of people of different origins, today's tourism is the engine that fuels this twenty-first century, bringing entirely new cultures and backgrounds to Nantucket's island population. For many islanders—natives and "washashores" alike—the island seems endangered. Prices are escalating, and people whose families have been here for generations face being unable to afford to live on island. Without this solid core of community, the center will not hold, and what will be lost is a vital part of what has always made Nantucket a special place.

But this is a community that continues to be a fulcrum for ideas, and those within it nurture a determined spirit that allows them to continue to find a way to stay.

When Mimi Beman talks about Nantucket, she refers to "a fourth wall"—a dimension that attempts to explain the ineffable: what is it about this island that grabs hold of our hearts and, for some, sinks an anchor in our souls? "It courses through your blood—this fourth wall—call it that, this infection of some kind. . . . It gets in your blood. The people who live here are completely in love and can't get it out of their system. People come here once a year, and they catch the bug. . . . It's the insularity and the community, those two things."

Nantucket's Oldest House.
Built in 1686 for a descendant of one of Nantucket's original settlers,
it was a wedding gift to Jethro Coffin and Mary Gardner.

Mimi adds, "It's the intersecting lives of people . . . the whole idea of being part of one thing—one thing that is shaped by the island's form; here we are, we are shaped by its form."

The very fact of its shape—this small island so far out to sea, bound by the ocean, a mere "elbow of sand" (as Melville had it) brings islanders closer, pulls in a sense of community. There's no getting off when a north-easter hits or a hurricane blows in. No planes will fly into stormy skies and no ferries will venture into those rough seas. There are plenty of days when fog, partially responsible for Nantucket's famous "Grey Lady" moniker, [it's the grey shingling that gave it the moniker, but it has also been attributed to fog] that makes air travel impossible and forces us to let go of any off-island schedule. It is to be cast into another century, where time and nature's seasons create a rhythm of their own. That does create an identity as an islander. You just can't leave. As Mimi continues, "And you adjust to that and you become a slightly different person because of it. Maybe you become more patient, maybe you learn to use other resources. Maybe you reach into yourself and pull out those resources."

Those who stay create a defining imprint of individuality within remarkable community. This island and its people are a treasure.

ISLAND INSTITUTIONS
Nantucket Bakeshop

To really understand the powerful pull of the Nantucket Bake Shop, come 'round midnight. The streets are quiet, lights are dimmed in the weathered, grey-shingled houses all along Orange Street; it's as if the covers are pulled up and the island is going to sleep. But there is one place where the lights are bright and the place is hopping. Draw close to the side kitchen door: classic rock and reggae music pulses. Welcome to 79 Orange Street. Owner Jay Detmer is just beginning his night shift as chief baker at this island institution.

The Nantucket Bake Shop opened in the early 1950s, when its original owner, Aime Poirier, converted the building from a small grocery store to become the first baker on Nantucket to offer what has become an island staple—Portuguese bread. The Bake Shop changed hands twice more: once to Joe Cecot, who ran the shop from 1965 to 1976, and then to Anne and David Bradt, who, in taking on the Bake Shop in 1976, introduced their daughter, Magee, and her husband, Jay Detmer, to the work—and the joy—of owning a business. It was a family partnership from the beginning. "It took the four of us to be able to run this business; we were all learning together," notes Magee. Until his death in 2005, Magee's father was the

bookkeeper. Today, her mother still helps prepare the specialty items, does the local grocery shopping, and pitches in anywhere that she is needed. "She's our No.1 Support Staff!" adds Magee, concluding, "Everybody's contribution is worthwhile, no matter how small."

What began as a lark—a way to stay on the island and work through the summers—turned into a life change. Magee and Jay became the fourth set of hands that worked to maintain what had become this island's tradition: a local, hands-on, baked-on-the- premises, old-fashioned bakery. Magee took over the management of the business and got to work learning the fundamentals of baking, turning out an array of products—from pies, cookies, and cupcakes to Nantucket favorites, such as almond macaroons, 'Sconset Sweets, and raspberry squares. Newly married when he and Magee first embarked on this enterprise, Jay found a calling. "I took a summer job and married the boss's daughter," he quips. He continues: "Just lucky to hit Nantucket—it's a beautiful place. I finally found that I was good at something—and I consider myself lucky to have found that out at a young age. Once you find something that you like and you're good at it, consider yourself blessed to be able to do it." Jay apprenticed with master baker and former owner Joe Cecot, learning the basics of bread baking; then, over the years, in the slower winter months, Jay traveled and worked with bakers from all over the world to develop and enlarge his mastery of the art of baking, including a stint at "D.D. University," better known as Dunkin' Donuts. Today, the Nantucket Bake Shop offers a selection of freshly baked breads—the classic Portuguese, cheddar cheese, sunflower oatmeal, and cinnamon raisin—as well as muffins, croissants, cookies, pies, and other pastries.

What draws many of us in that door early mornings are the doughnuts: plain, sugar, glazed (regular or chocolate), jelly-filled, cream-filled . . . in a word, delicious. Just as there is an art to baking bread, there is real artistry in the creation of all those doughnuts. Watching Jay knead the dough, put it through the sheeter, stamp out the individual doughnuts, fry them in batches, and finish them—filling them with cream or jelly, or glazing them with sugar or icing—is to observe what is surely a vanishing craft. There is nothing automated about the process here. Every item is created by hand and baked with care, watched over intently every step of the way.

Jay notes, "This is all hand-done, just as it was done fifty years ago." Most bake shops today are much more

mechanized; machines do the work that these human hands are doing, kneading the dough and hand-molding

bread, rolling out muffins and rolls, and hand-cutting doughnuts.

At the peak of the season, the summer months are buzzing with baking almost around the clock. The Bake

Shop opens at 6:30 in the morning, just as Jay and his group are finishing their night shift. Magee picks up

the daytime traffic, managing the daily business as well as baking throughout the day—finishing pies; decorat-

ing cakes; churning out summer cocktail staples like their traditional cheese sticks; and baking her namesake

cookie, the Magee, a chocolate lover's dream, rich with mocha, walnuts, and chocolate chips.

One childhood memory has even influenced the pricing: "When I was a kid, I would stand in line to buy a

loaf of Portuguese bread and I was allowed to use the change to buy myself a cupcake. So now, forty years

later, I will not raise the price of cupcakes above $1.10. I still want kids who're hanging onto that dollar and

some change to be able to come in and be able to get the one thing that's going to make them smile—a cup-

cake."

Magee Detmer

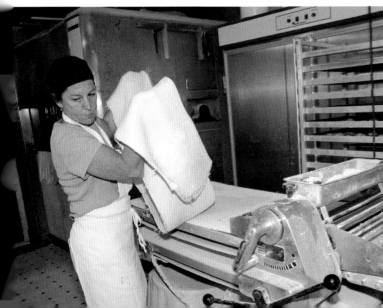

Willard Simpson

Lincoln Richards

Annecy Kagan

Congo Cookies

These are a longtime favorite for kids and grown ups. We like them best warm from the oven with a glass of milk.

Unsalted butter	6 ounces	Baking powder	1 1/2 tsp
Margarine	6 ounces	Salt	3/4 tsp
Oats	3 1/2 cups	Mini chocolate chips	1 cup
Sugar	1 1/2 cups	Raisins	1 cup
Brown sugar	2 cups	Pecans – chopped	1 cup
Eggs	3	Shredded coconut	3/4 cup
Vanilla extract	2 tsp	White chocolate or butterscotch chips	1 cup
Flour	3 cups		
Baking soda	1 1/2 tsp		

Preheat oven to 375°. Grind oats in food processor until powdery. Cream oats, butter, margarine, sugar and brown sugar in electric mixer. Add eggs and vanilla. Mix. Scrape bowl and mix again. Add flour, soda, baking powder, and salt. Mix. Add remaining ingredients and mix. Drop by heaping tablespoons on baking sheet lined with parchment (or lightly greased sheet) 2 inches apart. Bake 12 minutes.

Yields 6 dozen cookies.

At the height of summer, simply follow the trail of cars, bicycles, and pedestrians leading up to 50 Cliff Road, where the aroma of freshly baked bread wafts through the air. It's Something Natural, the island's best-known source for a range of fabulous oversized sandwiches, giant chocolate chip cookies, and a variety of artisanal breads.

Their breads are baked year round, and include the bestseller—Portuguese—a cultural touchstone derived from the heritage of the Portuguese fishermen and their families who began to come to America during the whaling era and settled in southeastern Massachusetts. Bread has always been a staple, and while the host of young Something Natural employees call out orders for sandwiches and assemble the delectable variety of ingredients, they are accompanied by the unmistakable hum and clatter of the bread slicer going through loaves of not just Portuguese but whole wheat, oatmeal, herb, rye, raisin, pumpernickel, and six grain breads.

For Matt Fee, Nantucket born and Harvard educated, coming back home to start a business was the only choice. "I am drawn to places where you can do more

Matt Fee

The Fee Family
Matt and Sheila, and twins Ruby and Henry.

GOOD THINGS TO EAT

During the winter months, Something Natural produces three to four hundred loaves of bread a day. Summer kicks it up more than a notch: this small shop works from early morning through the afternoon to get out fifteen hundred loaves of bread a day. "We work really hard, " says Matt. "Fourth of July to mid-August, we bake as much as a thousand cookies and three thousand loaves of bread a day."

"Baking is fun—baking bread, especially. There is a bit of an art to it. You know, pretty much within your shift, whether or not you've done a good job. There is a feeling of satisfaction when everything comes out right, when everything is done efficiently. You know it. When it doesn't work, you know it, too."

than one thing in a day." Having lived and worked in other cities, the idea of "getting up before the sun, getting in the suit, and coming home after the sun" held less appeal. "When I go off island, it strikes me how much time you spend commuting—bombarded with lights, sitting in a car. . . . Nantucket is the opposite of that. It is a manageable size. Here, you can do a few things in a day. You can have a meaningful impact. It feels like you're in a place that is self-sufficient, that is its own world."

Fee's father was a telephone lineman who grabbed the chance to open his own business: Henry's Sandwich Shop, which was the beginning of a series of businesses that he and his wife ran. There were lessons learned by young Matt. "I saw my parents make this change—and they did better when they were working for themselves."

Something Natural was an existing business that Matt bought in 1982. "One half of the recipes were existing. I already baked. I had worked for my dad at the Skipper (restaurant) on Steamboat Wharf. I gravitated to baking. I was a morning person anyway. There was a satisfaction. You knew right away if you did something right or not. I liked being behind the scenes. I baked for the sandwich shop and the restaurant. At sixteen, I was managing a staff of six to eight people. I worked all through my high school and college years."

While operating any business has its challenges, Something Natural has offered its own rewards: "It's the chance to produce a product that I'm proud of, and that people enjoy," offers Matt. "The part that has mattered is meeting the young people that I have worked with from all over the world. Those are compelling reasons to keep going."

"On Nantucket, you are never more than five minutes away from a place of singular beauty. And while working people must work hard and creatively to thrive here, the grace and solace of that beauty feels like a reward, some might say a blessing," says Annye Camara, owner of her namesake organic food market.

"As for this working person, service has always been the most satisfying part of any business I've owned. Here on island, serving a consistent (and growing) community of islanders is a deeper pleasure. Coming to know people over a span of years, learning about their lives, their families, their passions (their pets!)—Nantucket offers that in a unique way, by virtue of our being together on, well, an island. And, with a real boundary—the ocean—embracing us all, enmity is fleeting. Nantucketers quarrel, certainly, but I've never seen anything like when we all come together."

Annye Camara

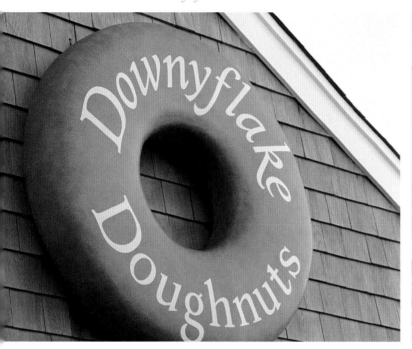

As you
Ramble on thru
Life brother—
whatever be you
goal— Keep
your eye upon
the doughnut
and not upon
the h le!

Carol Walsh and Norman Gauvin

Evie Sylvia with Susan Stephens and Charles "Chip" Hart.

Mother and daughter:
Bette Yarmy and Darrel Van Lieu

Owner Susan Tate Hogan

"Washashore" Norman Gauvin

"*Marine Home Center isn't about any one individual,*" *explains owner Denis Gazaille.* "*It takes a team of us to serve the community.*"

Jamie van Ecke, Michael Haigley, Jeremy Anderson, and Jim Cahill.

David Schwieger and Frank Andrade.

Mark Williams, Norman Gauvin, and Ted Strojny
Founders of the Demo Derby
(Photo Courtesy of Norman Gauvin)

"It's Demo time. It's the only thing we have left. It's just ours, no tourists.. Family and friends get together, play together, compete together and have fun." 2008 marks Demo Derby's 30th Anniversary.

Demo Derby photos courtesy of **The Nantucket Independent.**

Lucile Hays and Whitney Gifford

Bo Almodobar and Phyllis McInerney

Richard Glidden

As seventy percent of the island's elementary schoolchildren attend the programs, the Boys & Girls Club holds fast to its mission: "To enable all young people, especially those who need us most, to reach their full potential as productive, caring, responsible citizens."

"This little school is special because it's been in existence for the working people of Nantucket since 1969,"
reflects founder Jean Hughes. "These children are the third generation here. This is the community."

Bonnee Larsen, Chuck Gifford, Tina Moore, and Kim Horyn

Diane Pearl, M.D.

Margot Hartmann, M.D.

Greg Hinson, M.D.

Martha Lake Greenfield, Kathy Sossen, and Katie Joseph

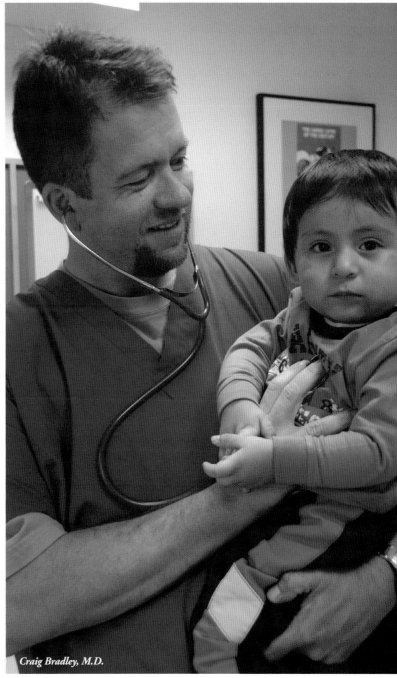
Craig Bradley, M.D.

Timothy Lepore, M.D. with daughter Meri Lepore, P.A.

Children's Medical Associates' Lou Arsenault

Veterinarian Bill Mentes, D.V.M.

Police Chief Randy Norris

Officer Bartlett

EMT and Fireman Jeffrey Allen

Fire Chief Bruce Watts

Founder Bambi Mleczko

Elliot Norton

John Bartlett

Photo courtesy of Jill Sandole and Bartlett's Ocean View Farm

The oldest continuously operating organization on island is the Union Lodge of Free and Accepted Masons of Nantucket, the second-oldest Masonic lodge in the nation, preceding the founding of the United States of America. A history written in 1941 by *Inquirer and Mirror* editor Harry B. Turner states that Nantucket's Union Lodge F. & A. M. was established by charter on May 27, 1771, in the town that was still called Sherburne. The charter was granted following a petition addressed to the Provincial Grand Master of the Ancient and Honorable Society of Free and Accepted Masons for all North America, whose headquarters was in Boston. The petition was submitted and signed by six Nantucket men—all Masons, all mariners—who requested "that if it is consistent with your will and pleasure, that you would send us a warrant so that we may have a just and perfect lodge consecrated here. . . . "

The history of the organization of Masons and the values and traditions celebrated harkens to their beginnings as the original stonemason guilds operating throughout medieval England. These guilds served as important connectors to the highly skilled craftsmen who plied their trade building the great cathedrals, castles, and monuments, but who necessarily traveled and lived in different communities as they worked. The guilds ensured that the highest standards and values would be met, as well as serving as important links to their fellow stonemasons. The term "freemason" derives from the name and quality of the freestone, which was a stone that could be cut without splitting, as well as being soft enough to allow intricate carving.

2007-2008 Master, Wardens and Officers

Photo courtesy of James McIntosh

Throughout the Age of Enlightenment in the eighteenth century, these standards and traditions, values and order came to be applied to the construct of building character in man. Freemasonry became a fraternity based on the "fatherhood of God and the brotherhood of man," using allegorical and symbolic frameworks from stonemasonry to cement the ideals and foundation of the organization. Masons have played their part in U. S. history: nine Freemasons signed the Declaration of Independence; ten signed the Constitution; and fourteen Masons have been our nation's president. Paul Revere, who was to become the Grand Master of the Grand Lodge of Massachusetts, was a silversmith who crafted the original "jewels" of the Nantucket Union Lodge—three solid silver badges of Masonic office representing the "level," the "plumb," and the "square" worn by early island officers, and treasured by island Masons today.

Nantucket's chapter continues this ancient tradition—joining men of various faiths, levels of education, and professions—in adhering to the tenets of Masonry by vowing to "meet on the level, act on the plumb, and part on the square." This fraternity of men holds true to timeless and enduring values of "taking a good man and making him better" and continues to be an integral part of the community—in its charitable nature, focusing on the needs of the seriously and terminally ill, as well as connecting the bonds of brothers. Original members were whaling captains, simple mariners, and prominent merchants; representative members today are islanders Daniel Bartlett of Bartlett's Oceanview Farm; Maurice Gibbs, Commodore of the Wharf Rat Club; and scrimshander Charles Manghis.

The distinctive insignia found on the Wharf Rat burgees and pins came from the wildly creative imagination of designer Tony Sarg, a beloved figure on-island.

Come by Old North Wharf on a summer or fall morning, to a former fishing shanty, and glimpse a bit of Nantucket's private world: the Wharf Rat Club members sitting around, sharing stories and a laugh. This is a members-only club, welcoming visitors, but honoring the code of entry: a good story and a modest demeanor. Character counts here.

Founded in 1926, the Wharf Rats got their start by the location of this cedar-shingled shack on the water. North Wharf was a functioning mooring for boats that were privately owned as well as those that were available for rent. Quahog fishermen were aplenty in the early days of the twentieth century, as the storms of the late nineteenth century had created a "haul-over" in the upper harbor, where large beds of quahogs were discovered in Nantucket Harbor. A thriving fishery also engendered a small chandlery, where fishing and boating supplies and necessities such as oilskins, boots, and warm gear could be acquired.

It was a natural progression for this spot to become a hangout for fishermen. Gathering around a pot-bellied stove on cold, foggy mornings, waiting for the sun to rise before getting under way, the camaraderie and friendship established bonds that were formalized with the creation of a new social institution, which they dubbed the "Wharf Rat Club," after the small rodent known for infesting wharves and ships.

Paul Clarke with Reginald Reed, member of fifty years' standing.
Mr. Reed's father was the last lighthouse keeper at Brant Point.

Bob Erskine with Commodore Maurice Gibbs

What does it take to be a Wharf Rat? If you say, "I want to be a Wharf Rat," the current commodore, retired U. S. Navy Commander Maurice Gibbs cautions with a big laugh: "Don't ever walk in the door and say that! You have to be brought in here by a Rat. Name of the game is, you come here for a period of three years or more, you fit in, and suddenly someone says, well, I think she's a Wharf Rat, or someone says no, and so they may make her or him one. Both male and female, there are Rats of both genders."

"Cross this threshold . . . the motto of this club is NO RESERVED SEATS FOR THE MIGHTY. Which means, when you cross this threshold, we don't care what walk of life you came out of, or what your status is, or anything. In here, there is no status except friendship. One's station in life is of no consequence. One's character is."

A singular exception was made in June of 1933. An unexpected summer squall blew in President Franklin D. Roosevelt, who had been headed to Provincetown from Martha's Vineyard. Although the President never stepped foot on land, staying on his boat in the harbor, the town celebrated his arrival. The Wharf Rats instantly declared him an honorary member. Commodore Coffin approached the presidential schooner *Amberjack II* with the gift of the trademark triangular flag, known as a "burgee," with its distinctive insignia of a pipe-smoking Wharf Rat against a marine blue background. And as the President sailed off early the next morning, the Wharf Rat pennant was flying proudly aloft the presidential craft.

Through the decades, there have been many notable members. But that's not what counts. What matters is the rare spirit of genuine friendship and affection; it's all about conversation and stories—good stories. That's the price of admission.

Reverend Patricia Barrett and Reverend Joel Ives

Philip Jekanowski and Father Paul Green

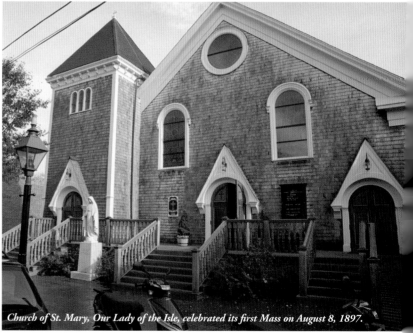

Church of St. Mary, Our Lady of the Isle, celebrated its first Mass on August 8, 1897.

St. Paul's Church has ministered to the island's Episcopalians for over 150 years.

Established as a school in the 1820s, this small building became the spiritual and cultural center for the African American community.

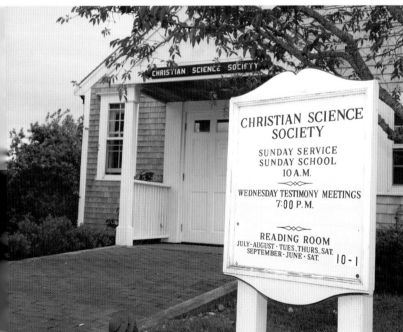

The Christian Science Society observing the centrality of "healing prayer based on spiritual law" celebrates the words of founder, Mary Baker Eddy: "The depth, breadth, height, might, majesty, and glory of infinite love fill all space. That is enough!"

A congregation of diverse religious beliefs and traditions, Unitarian Universalists have as a central tenet "respect for the inherent worth of every person."

ISLAND INSTITUTIONS
The Inquirer and Mirror

Nantucket's oldest newspaper, the *Inquirer and Mirror,* continues to roll off the presses much like the news-papers of yesterday—the large broadsheet pages a vestige of American newspaper publishing's golden age. Although rival newspapers have surfaced across the generations, only one has published the news of this community week in and week out since its inception in 1821.

At the helm of history, editor and publisher Marianne Stanton continues not only the newspaper's tradition but that of her own family. Stanton was raised in the newspaper business as her parents, Marie and Tom Giffin, bought the *Inquirer and Mirror* in the late 1960s. At thirteen, Marianne got her first taste of the news business, working behind the scenes all through high school. She came back as a reporter in 1981 and was named editor in 1985. In 1990, the Giffin family sold the *Inquirer and Mirror* to Ottaway Community Newspapers, which had been a division of Dow Jones & Co. until its sale in late 2007 to Rupert Murdoch's News Corporation. Marianne continued as editor and publisher through both sales.

Continuing to operate as an independent company, the *Inky Mirror,* as islanders affectionately dub it, has been the newspaper of record for the island, and an editorial voice that has championed the needs and concerns of the community.

The Nantucket Independent has trod where other newspapers have faltered. Veteran newsman and reporter Don Costanzo founded the paper in July 2003, and was joined in the publishing venture shortly thereafter by Dan Drake, who had spent a career in banking.

The mission was to create another voice for the island, another prism through which islanders could obtain coverage of local news and issues of the day. The *Independent* — Nantucket's only locally owned weekly newspaper — prides itself on editorial experience and perspective. "It's our ability to think outside the box and to think forward creatively," explains Costanzo, editor and publisher. "We have a core, experienced staff of reporters and editors."

Drake, associate publisher, looks on the operation as offering "a more balanced view of the community. The paper makes every effort to show where things need fixing, but tries to focus on the positive aspects." Further, he adds: "The key is each person bringing his or her own piece of the whole puzzle, if you will, of putting the newspaper together."

A true business partnership, all major decisions are made together. But there is a division of duties. "The way I see it, my role is to run the business side of the paper, everything from bookkeeping to newspaper

The Nantucket Real Estate Guide ◆ Section 3

THE NANTUCKET Independent

THE ISLAND'S LOCALLY OWNED WEEKLY SOURCE FOR NEWS, BUSINESS AND THE ARTS

Volume 5, Number 18 • Nantucket, MA 02554   *November 7, 2007 • Free • www.acknews.com*

Building a place for Vets to call home

BY MARY LANCASTER
INDEPENDENT WRITER

Veterans seek longer lease to secure new post

With luck, the new Veterans of Foreign Wars Post 8608 will open next year on Bunker Road in a 158-foot-long building that will be nearly three times the size of the former headquarters, complete with air conditioning, a sprinkler system and a commercial kitchen.

It has been next to impossible to find a place to gather the VFW's 100-plus members since about six years ago when the original

See VETERANS, page 3

THE DRIVE
Whalers win on the final play of the game to mark homecoming finale.
PAGE 27

ODD FELLOWS
Venerable organization to install new officers Saturday.
PAGE 12

INSIDE
three sections

QUOTABLE

"If our country is worth dying for in time of war, let us resolve that it is truly worth living for in time of peace."

~ Hamilton Fish

PHOTOS BY ROB BENCHLEY/The Independent

Homes and dunes at the end of Massachusetts Avenue near Smith's Point took a pasting during Saturday's storm; the sloop "Boru," one of a dozen boats that slipped their moorings, came ashore hard against the pier at 64 Monomoy Road

Noel, hurricane-turned-nor'easter, hammers island

ConCom issues enforcement orders on imperiled Madaket homes

After morphing into a powerful nor'easter, the remnants of Hurricane Noel pounded and soaked Nantucket with 87-mph gusts and nearly four inches of rain on Saturday.

The large, fast-moving storm — which lost its hurricane status as it worked its way up the coast through increasingly cooler waters last week — washed away more than 20 feet of

BY PETER B. BRACE
INDEPENDENT WRITER

shoreline in Madaket, blew boatloads of scallops up onto harbor beaches and downed two large American elms on North Water Street.

Although the National Weather Service office in Taunton, Mass. listed gusts to 72 mph

around 6:30 p.m. on Saturday, local reports put island wind gusts as high as 87 mph.

"As it moved up the coast, it lost its tropical characteristics. Basically it was just a very powerful nor'easter," said National Weather Service Meteorologist Charley Foley. "It did

See NOEL, page 14

Bountiful scallop harvest greets island fishermen

BY PETER B. BRACE
INDEPENDENT WRITER

Scalloper Marty Mack said jokingly over the weekend as he collected storm-beached scallops off the shore along Hulbert Avenue that the bay scallop fishery is crashing — crashing into his dredges, that is.

Although Mack was partly referring to the bonanza of scallops that Saturday's nor'easter blew onto harbor beaches, his early commercial season sentiment is also that of other long-time fishermen who see a decidedly more bountiful five months of scalloping in front of them.

"With the number of boats that I'm seeing, it should be a very good year for

See SCALLOPS, page 5

PHOTO BY BARBARA GOOKIN

Hank Garnett, who fishes with his sister Evie Sylvia, offloads their 10 boxes of scallops caught within three hours.

LEADING LADIES
AN INDEPENDENT SERIES · PART 5

WOMEN IN BUSINESS

BY MARY LANCASTER
INDEPENDENT WRITER

Whether working at manual labor, selling goods or in the field of beauty, people doing business on Nantucket have to be adept at determining how to cover the demands of the summer season and weather the slow months of winter. The island's women seem to be very good at that, building their businesses to the point they desire and then maintaining that level despite a fluctuating economy. This week we spoke with five Nantucket businesswomen who share their success with many peers in all sectors of the community.

VICKI GOSS

Some of Goss's clients have been astonished at her ability to do what many view as heavy work — men's work. But Goss, who is one of the island's prominent female landscapers, does not shrink from hard labor, including laying stone patios, and is a skilled and respected gardener who takes great pride in her

See LEADING LADIES, page 11

Don Costanzo and Daniel Drake

Editor's note: *The Nantucket Independent* was acquired by GateHouse Media in April 2008.
"This acquisition will provide *The Independent* with the resources it needs to take it to the next level," said founder
Don Costanzo. "Our readers can be assured that GateHouse will sustain and enhance a tradition that began not more
than five years ago with little more than an idea and a passion."

sales, to taking out the garbage (laughs) . . . everything that goes along with it," says Drake. "Don oversees the reporters, giving them guidance on their writing, guidance on stories they should be covering, and his sort of 'taking out the garbage role' is laying out the paper and everything that goes into getting the paper to the printer every week."

The paper takes a particular interest in profiling businesses and the people within them, while recognizing the importance of having another forum for representation. "For me it was more than just creating an editorial voice. It was creating another vehicle for businesses to advertise. The newspaper monopoly created by Ottaway (then owner of the *Inquirer and Mirror*) provided just one weekly advertising vehicle. That wasn't fair to the businesses on this island," Costanzo said. "We've changed that, in a lot of ways."

In answer to the question: What do you hope your newspaper represents to this community?

Don: *"What I'd like is for people to see the **Independent** as something that offered an alternative. I don't want to view us as the savior, or the other option to the **I&M**. But we hope we are the voice for Nantucket. Something that people turn to every week for news and information. We provide information objectively, giving you issues and development plans so you can think for yourself."*

Dan: *"I would only add to that something that I've said in bits and pieces. First, we give as fair and balanced a representation of the community as we can; and, second, that it (the paper) makes people think. The hope is that it provokes thought and discussion. The paper is really a catalyst for community action, if you will, in the broadest sense, not in a narrow sense."*

Nantucket Historical Association

Perhaps nothing speaks to the idea of small-town life more than the very idea of bartering: exchanging one set of goods or services for another. Here on Nantucket that tradition continues within the stories of three families and businesses—all of which have been chronicled in these pages.

For Bill and Ruth Blount, raising seven children on a fisherman's salary was a challenge that required looking back to a tradition that hearkens to Nantucket's earliest days, when English settlers would trade and exchange information and goods for crops and food, as well as help from the Native Americans. The early years of Colonial America were founded on the principles of bartering, as coins were scarce and the colonists' currency became what could be traded. Fur pelts—such as beaver, otter, and deer; crops—such as corn or wheat; and hand-hewn products—such as nails—were tradable commodities.

Bill and Ruth Blount, Anne and David Brady with their daughter, Magee Detmer

Today, fisherman Bill Blount and his wife, Ruth, look to Bartlett's Ocean View Farm and the Nantucket Bake Shop to round out their family's needs. Trading freshly caught flounder and cod for fruits and vegetables and freshly baked goods makes for an abiding sense of belonging to that larger family of man.

"We have lived here thirty-three years, and some of those years have been lean ones. But they've been rich in the sense of how the community has cared for us. I've always said that if I have to be in crisis somewhere, I want it to be on Nantucket.

Bartering has been a part of our family ever since I met Bill. I've told Bill that other men bring their wives emeralds, and he brings me bushels of broccoli or quahogs! So our riches have been in our children, our faith, our neighbors, and good food!

I deeply hope that the friends we have bartered with through these years have been equally satisfied with the arrangement. We have always tried to be more than fair. But I do remember many times when our boat was in dry dock for months at a time, totally out of commission, and our bartering "rights" continued right on through. It's been more of a trust between neighbors than just a business arrangement."

Ruth Blount

Photo courtesy of Rob Benchley

Bill Blount, Phil Bartlett, Ruth Blount, Dorothy Bartlett

As it is in many small towns, high-school football continues to be a unifying element of this community, at least since Vito Capizzo came to town. One life can touch so many others, and Vito's life plays like a scene from the film classic, *It's a Wonderful Life.*

Vito Capizzo is a legend in his own time, at least in this town of Nantucket. He is widely credited with turning around the very idea of sports for the island children, creating not just an exemplary football program but establishing a variety of middle school and junior varsity sports teams and, in the process, creating a community of parents and students who stay connected through generations.

Now in his forty-fourth season of coaching, he is touching the lives of the third and fourth generations of Nantucket families he has served. He is credited by many for using the game and training for football to help train these young athletes for life. When he first arrived on island, as a young man of twenty-three in 1964, fourteen boys showed up for that first practice, and prospects looked dismal. "I came home, told my wife, 'Don't unpack. Let's get the hell out of here.' It was impossible to put a team together. I had to be patient. I was young, high strung, I wanted to win more than the kids did." That first year the newly formed team lost all but one game, which was a tie. But the trajectory of change had started. The second year brought one win. "I told the kids, 'You gotta believe in yourself and you gotta do it.' No such phrase, 'I can't do it.' I had to convey that to my team. The third year, we came together as a team and as a family and we were undefeated. The whole town went crazy."

The team en route to a game off island, via the ferry.

Turning a team into winners brought pride and a sense of community to Nantucket, but Vito's coaching style and vision for these kids changed their lives. "He turned them around," says Andy (Andrea) Marks, islander for the past thirty-eight years and a mother. "People had few expectations for their kids . . . kids who had been told that they weren't college material. Vito took them off-island to see schools, he counseled them, and gave hope to the kids who were told that college wasn't really for them."

Loyalty and passion for their coach runs strong: "When Vito got here, we had no football program to speak of; he turned a losing team into a winning team. The community got behind him. Kids cannot wait to get with Vito. He got a program going—and it's a winning program. The kids love him, the parents love him; he's a great coach. Vito could go out for mayor and he'd be elected," comments longtime islander Norman Gauvin, parent and ten-year volunteer in the Booster Club, an organization that Vito established to help fund the team and raise spirits. When asked how Coach Capizzo managed to make that difference, Norman responded, "He took every kid to heart. The kids respected him and knew he cared. He helped a lot of kids get on to the mainland and get into school. He has touched many hearts and touched many families."

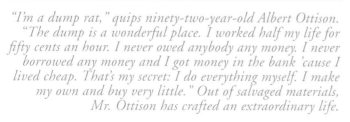

"I'm a dump rat," quips ninety-two-year-old Albert Ottison. "The dump is a wonderful place. I worked half my life for fifty cents an hour. I never owed anybody any money. I never borrowed any money and I got money in the bank 'cause I lived cheap. That's my secret: I do everything myself. I make my own and buy very little." Out of salvaged materials, Mr. Ottison has crafted an extraordinary life.

The sisters' trademark pose: See no evil, speak no evil, hear no evil...

Sisters Nancy Chase, Phyllis Chase Burchell, and Susan Chase Ottison.
In 1690, James Chase arrived on-island from Martha's Vineyard; other branches
of the family thread back to Abiah Folger, Benjamin Franklin's mother.

The Ray Family, which includes the Barrett, the Williams, the Appleton, and Morris families, some of which descended from Nantucket's founding Coffin family. Most branches of the Ray family stretch back some twelve to fifteen generations.

Left to right: Anna Dickie, Evie Sylvia, Hank Garnett, Irene Garnett, Gail Anderson, and Rene Conrad

Four Generations

Chris Fuller

Lizbet Fuller and Son Eli

Andrea "Andy" Marks and Son Tristram "Tris" Marks

(Dog: Amy)   Chris Van der Wolk, Bob Brickley, Carl Sjolund

Tharon Dunn

Eleanor *"Miss Ellie"* Ferreira

Wendy Mills and Ursula McMorrow of *The Camera Shop*

TELLER

EXPRESS·ONE ITEM

349

Jonathan Anastos with his dog, Kodi.

Darcy Creech

Darcy Creech devised a winning formula to break bad habits in people of all ages and all walks of life with *Habit-Patch Quit Kits*—a ten-step program that uses witty patches and gentle humor to open the door of communication and get relationships back on track. "Habit-Patch," says founder Darcy Creech, "is on a mission to revolutionize relationships—one Quit Kit at a time. It's only by addressing a person's behavior with an attitude of non judgment and encouragement that you can help them out of their rut. Helping people see the truth without putting them on the defensive, however, is an art form. When it comes to curing social malaise, we are happy to report that laughter can move mountains."

Elin Hilderbrand

Best-selling author Elin Hilderbrand found fertile ground for launching a writing career. Nantucket is the inspiration and locale for a range of books exploring relationships and lives lived on this island. "I write about Nantucket," explains Hildebrand, "not only because it is my home, but because it is one of the few authentic places left in America. I am inspired by the impeccably preserved historic downtown, the pristine beaches and moors, and most of all, by the people who value these things as much as I do. And of course, on an island thirty miles out to sea, there is no shortage of interesting stories. . . ."

Larry Belka

Ella and Amy England

"Nantucket holds so much appeal for families; it is less about corporate life and more about family and community. I made this choice in raising my own family," reflects Bartlett's Farm Sales & Marketing Director, Larry Belka. "Working at Bartlett's Farm, which is the epitome of an island family, centers on trying to meet the direct needs of the community and supporting people who live and work on the island. Supporting local has significance because what we grow and make at the farm stays on the island. Farm-grown and farm-made is real and is at the core of what we do here."

Singer and songwriter Amy England and daughter Ella. Her latest album, *From Nantucket to Nashville,* is inspired by the beauty of this seaside town. "I am drawn to seaside towns and small communities. Winter is found time to write songs, you can gather everything together. The darkness of the season makes you dig deep for emotional things. You can see that up close with a small community...see into other people's relationships. Maybe more than they'd want you to," England says with a laugh. "But it's great fodder. Some of the best songs have been written in sad times."

Jean Duarte

David and Anne Bradt

Anita Nettles Stefanski

Beverly Hall

Sam Slosek and Rachel Starbuck Slosek with their daughter, Sophia.

Rachel is descended from one of Nantucket's founding settlers, Edward Starbuck. The Starbuck family was one of the island's most influential of the nineteenth-century, becoming successful merchants through ownership of a fleet of whaling ships, which brought the riches of millions of gallons of whale oil, which was processed and sold, as well as the production of candles made from spermaceti. At the height of the whaling trade, the family business of cordage and cooper shops was booming. Joseph Starbuck, one of the most prosperous island men, decided to ensure his three sons' place, not only in the business, but in the sense of family solidarity, by building three identical brick houses on Main Street. Emerson, who was visiting the island in 1834, upon witnessing the imposing Three Bricks, wrote in his diary: "What is there of the divine in a load of bricks…Much. All." "I am the eighth generation of Starbucks to live in this house," remarks Rachel. "Traditionally, the house has been passed down to the women in the family. I'm the next in line, the only child from both my dad and uncle so that would leave me as steward of the house. And now I have a daughter…Sophia Starbuck Slosek."

The Three Bricks

William Starbuck born the 6th month 27th 173
Mary Starbuck born the 3th month 6th 17

Their Children

Kezia Starbuck born 6th 1st day 1756
William Starbuck born 6th 26th 1756
He deceased at or near New York the 1st mo 1779
Phebe Starbuck born the 4th month 11th 1758
Deceased 9th month the 22 nd 1759
Elisabeth Starbuck born 8th mo the 7th 1760
Deceased 2 nd mo the 28th 1786
Judeth Starbuck born 9th mo the 14th 1762
Heil Starbuck born 11th month the 3 1764
Deceased 5th mo the 18th 1786
Caban Starbuck born 11th mo the 25 th 1766 De
A Daughter born 7th mo the 16th 1769 Died sce
Kimball Starbuck born 1st mo 22 nd 1771
Amanda Starbuck born 10th mo 3 1773
Lydia Starbuck born 11th mo the 28 th 1777
Deceased 11th mo the 20th 1810
Aishu Starbuck born 2 nd mo 3 1780

Lita Toland and her son Rory

Jim Lentowski

"I've been in the same position for thirty-seven years," laughs Jim Lentowski, Executive Director of the **Nantucket Conservation Foundation**. "My arrival in 1971 immediately followed the foundation's first purchase of land, the Ram Pasture property, that was later added to by the Sanford Farm property. Today, we have nine thousand acres that are protected. The legacy carried forward is the protection of the character and nature of these natural landscapes that remain the heart of the island."

Wendy Hudson

"We are so lucky to have made amazing strides in terms of preserving Nantucket's history and open space. At **Sustainable Nantucket** we work to help shape the island's future in a positive way with the hope that similar success will be felt in preserving our community character and quality of life," reflects Board Chair Wendy Hudson. "It's a fragile system, but happily we have an incredibly high number of people who care very deeply about this special place."

Marie "Ralph" Henke

Elizabeth "Libby" Oldham

"Although this little speck of sand is constantly undergoing development pressures, it remains a truly unique island. Every trip to America brings this point sharply into focus," an apt phrase coming from the **Nantucket Historical Association's Research Library** Photograph Specialist, Marie "Ralph" Henke. "The insulated small-town life is good for your health. People take care of each other in times of difficulty."

"After some thirty years of year-round living on Nantucket, I'm planted," says Elizabeth "Libby" Oldham, Research Associate at the **Nantucket Historical Association's Research Library**. A beloved figure on island, she was recognized by an appreciative friend in a dedicatory plaque bolted to a bench outside the library that reads "The Seat of All Wisdom." "Having just turned eighty-one," Libby muses, "I feel singularly blessed to be still functioning and cherishing my days and nights here, and there is still 'nowhere else on earth that I would rather be.' "

WAMPANOAG WAY

VILLAGE OF MADAKET

SURFSIDE

SIASCONSET

TOM NEVERS

NANTUCKET STEAMSHIP WHARF

Travel eight miles eastward from the town center of Nantucket and you will reach the outermost area of the island, the secluded spot of Siasconset, commonly known as 'Sconset. The name evokes the island's Native American history as well as its whaling past, for it is roughly translated as "place of many bones." Originally a fishing village, peppered with rustic fishing shacks, the arrival of railway service in 1890 brought a fresh influx of islanders looking for a respite from the crowded town. Larger summer cottages were built, and advertisements for the simpler charms of 'Sconset brought a tide of new visitors, a sizable number drawn from New York's theater set. A thriving actors colony soon set a new standard for this tiny resort community.

'S c o n s e t

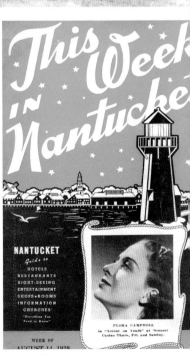

E p i l o g u e

366

History, like a vast river, propels logs, vegetation, rafts, and debris; it is full of live and dead things, some destined for resurrection; it mingles many waters and holds in solution invisible substances stolen from distant soils. Anything may become part of it; that is why it can be an image of the continuity of mankind.

Jacques Barzun
Historian, Philosopher, Author

History has charted these waters and the history of man on this soil. From J. Hector St. John de Crèvecoeur's 1782 *Letters from an American Farmer,* to Nantucket's Obed Macy's 1835 *History of Nantucket* and Alexander Starbuck's 1924 seminal *History of Nantucket: Island, County, and Town,* to Edouard Stackpole's numerous publications, to the chronicling of our past and future from current Nantucket historians Nathaniel Philbrick, Robert F. Mooney, and Frances Ruley Karttunen. Nantucket continues to weave its stories into the fabric of this town.

It is a tide of humanity that has swept upon these shores and left its mark on the lives that play out today. Be mindful that our mark is on the future.
Tread carefully.

Dedication

This book never would have begun without the Bradley family. David's invitation to visit, twenty-eight years ago, was the introduction to this island. With their characteristic grace, David and his parents, Mary Ann "Terri" and Gene Bradley, and his sister, Barbara, welcomed us to their home. Nantucket has been my safe harbor ever since—a place I know my soul resides.

Through these years, with the addition of Katherine and the birth of the boys, the Bradley family has been the constant in our lives, the anchor and port in every storm and the truest friends of life.

Terri Bradley, Robert Haft, Gene Bradley, David Bradley, Barbara Bradley

The Bradley Family: (sitting) Carter, Mrs. Bradley, Adam, and Katherine
(standing) Spencer and David

Acknowledgments

This book has changed shape and form and found its way through the help of a few important individuals:

Steven Rales, who quite literally gave me wings and the chance to let this book fly.
Chris Fuller, who was my guide and helpmate on the water; those were golden days.
And to *Albert Glowacki* and in memory of *Gary Glowacki*, who introduced our family to the joys and freedom of escaping by sea.

Darryl Carter, who by example and by design led the way for inspiration and hope and showed me the way to believe that this idea and this vision could be made real.
Charles Grazioli, whose constant admonishment: *Get to Work!* (said half in jest) and constant encouragement, as well as hardworking example, was a necessary lifeline.
And to *Barbara Harrison*, leading the charge—in life and in friendship.
To *Nancy Seaman*, love and loyalty know no bounds.
And to two women who have been lifetime inspirations: across the street, *Letitia "Tish" Baldrige*; and "across the pond," *Shirley Conran.*

My design team of *Eduardo Garcia, Daniel Troconis, Catalina Torres,* and *Roberto Sablayrolles*—who made this vision a reality and gave shape and design to ideas. But beyond their design expertise, their companionship and camaraderie breathed life and spirit into these pages.
To *Bob Barnett,* it is a blessing to be on your list.
Mimi Beman, who was the first person I turned to, and whose lifetime speaks to the very idea of what matters here with community and connection. She was unstinting with advice and encouragement and then led me to Libby Oldham.
My editor, *Elizabeth "Libby" Oldham*, who took my breath away with her skillful finesse and graceful art of editing, while providing a ballast of wisdom, counsel, and encouragement.
Having ploughed through every volume of photographs at the NHA Research Library, *Marie "Ralph" Henke,* provided an experienced eye and wise judgment, as well as steady encouragement (and laughter!).

To *Jean Halberstam*, whose early shop helped my island house become a home and whose generosity of spirit in sharing the memories of her husband, David, with his love of fishing and the sea, and in sharing a photograph that was special to them.
And to *Wendy Hudson, Don Costanzo,* and *Chuck Gifford*, helpmates and springboards—always responsive for which I am forever grateful.
Happiness was found in hours spent at the *Atheneum* and at the *NHA Research Library;* two institutions that should be prized and protected.
And succor, support, and friendship always found at 21 Federal with *Pam Raith* and *Robert Sarkisian* (which began with *Chick and Mary Walsh).*

The foundation of family is the wellspring from which this book took shape.

To my husband and my children, who probably thought this day would never come—their love is my constant, and source of my strength.

To my twin sister, *Maura,* my lifetime sounding board, and the other beat of my heart. Credit her with the subtitle, which, of course, is perfect.

To my father, *Dr. William Zeiler,* whose principles of dedication, hard work, and achievement, particularly in service to others, is the lesson I continue to carry. And to the memory of my mother, *Geraldine Colby Zeiler,* whose faith and humanity continue to be grace notes in my life. And to my brother, *Billy,* whose abiding love of family and reunion matter more than he knows. And to *Gerry,* whose loyalty and love are immeasurable. And to *Nita,* whose literary heart and loyal soul is a gift.

And to my mother-in-law, *Gloria Haft Furman,* who has shown me the bedrock of fierce love, loyalty, and devotion, for which I am forever blessed. And to my sister-in-law, *Linda Haft,* who is a living example of courage and tenacity, and most of all, love.

371